Althar Intense
Space – Time – Veiling

Joachim Wolffram

Also available from Joachim Wolffram:
"For You – Records from Your Lives"
"The Free Human"

The Althar series:
Volume 1: "Althar – The Crystal Dragon"
Volume 2: "Althar – The New Magi"
Volume 3: "Althar – Towards Utopia"
Volume 4: "Althar – The Final Letting Go"
Volume 5: "Althar – Opus Magnum"

**For information about audio recordings
and workshops please visit:**
www.wolffram.de

or

facebook.com/joachim.wolffram

Contents

Preface

The following text is a transcript of the live messages Althar and Aouwa gave at a workshop in Cascais/Lisbon, Portugal, in March 2019. In some places, the grammar or sentence structure has been corrected and occasionally one or the other word has been added to make a statement clearer.

As a transcript cannot adequately reflect the actual dynamics and atmosphere during the sessions, the audio recordings of this event can be purchased at www.wolffram.de. These are specifically helpful for diving into the guided meditations and the light body exercise.

1. Introduction – Eye of Suchness – True Encounter

I am Aouwa.

I am the absolute – a true self in expression. I am the relative – a human in expression. And I am the mystery in-between that connects both. I am three, and I am one, and I am so much more, just as you are.

It is, once again, a great delight for me to greet you here and to finally see you in the physical. But as you might have felt, you are not only here in physical form. You are also here with your true self and everything that connects your true self to what you perceive as the physical.

Within pure consciousness, there is *absolutely no separation*. That means it contains *no levels whatsoever*. So, when I speak of the absolute and the relative and the in-between, then I am already diving towards you. Into the world of separation, into the world of fabricated illusions. Why do we do this? Because the only way, so it seems, to get *out* of the world of separation, to get *out* of the world of illusion, is to apply *other* illusions to dissolve the illusions. It is like... imagine you have a thorn in your skin, and it hurts, it's painful. You want to remove this thorn, so you might use another thorn to pull the first one out. Once the thorn is removed and the pain is gone, you have two thorns which are both equal. There is not one good thorn and one bad. They are just made up things, made up means: illusionary – and you can let go of both of them.

So, whatever happens here is an attempt to find *appropriate* illusions to heal you from illusions. Because you have been so long in the world of separation, in the realms of separation, because you have experienced so much, because you have piled up so many beliefs, so many traumas, and fears, it is quite an effort to get rid of all of that. So, we need some *masterful* illusions. That is why we gather here.

Whatever we will do here, be it in this workshop or even in the future to come, will be based on three pillars.

The first pillar is *true wisdom*. There is the common wisdom that tells you how to behave with other people. If you have some experience, you know how things work out, and you know how to serve polarity. This is a kind of common place wisdom, which is fine, which makes you feel good, which allows you to behave more appropriately in the world of separation. But true wisdom is the wisdom that allows you to *go beyond*, that allows you to *liberate* yourself. This is true wisdom.

True wisdom so often comes first from other people in a form of a mental concept. Not always, but quite often. You hear expressions like "true self", or "letting go", or "separation is not real". It might be difficult at first, but at some point, you might accept it. But still, it is yet a way to really experience it from within. So, bringing the concept of true wisdom into a *lived experience* is what makes true wisdom a true potency. A potency that allows you to truly let go, to *truly see things as they really are*. So, true wisdom is pillar number one and making it a lived experience is what we are trying to allow.

The second pillar is a very difficult one. It is called *practice*. And practice is something that the human typically misunderstands. The human is *totally* conditioned to always try to *achieve* something by *doing* something. If he is not good enough for something, then he has to train, he has to improve, he has to perfect himself until he masters a certain skill or is able to create something of importance. This is all the upbringing, all the socialization of the human. So, when the term practice comes up, images come along with it. Such as doing some of the martial arts where you get certain belts in certain colors, you practice your katas and all the rest, and then at some point, you're good enough to wear a nice belt. Some can have a black one or a red one or whatever it is, and you feel great and wonderful. But the practice I'm talking about has *nothing at all* to do with that! In a sense, the practice we are providing and investigating here *is already true wisdom*. The practice in itself that is enlightenment.

It means shifting your perspective into a state where you really know: *Enlightenment is your natural state,* and you just stay there. The practice, the true practice that we are doing here, is *not a doing*, it is a *not-doing*. A not-doing! It is deconditioning. You see, deconditioning is so crucial, because it is all the conditioning, all the patterns that drive you through your daily life and that drive you from lifetime to lifetime.

The practice, the true practice of awakening means: Shift your perspective instantly and *see things as they truly are.*

You are *not* what you can perceive, you are not the patterns, you can just observe them. This is a non-practice, because you do nothing. Observation is not a doing; it is a natural given. So, this is true practice, and as you know, you *cannot create enlightenment.* That's why all the practice you might do in the classical sense is *absolutely* in vain. It brings you *nothing* other than that you're going in circles. It might bring you nice experiences, of course, it might lead you to nice people, of course, but in terms of enlightenment, well, it is not truly helpful. To practice is the second pillar.

The third pillar is *compassion.* Compassion is what you need the most when you are on the way to enlightenment, specifically when you are on your last steps into enlightenment. When you first hear about this, when you hear the call from within, then it is all exciting and new. You have a lot of insights and experiences. Things are opening up, and your daily life might change drastically. But then, as you move on and you feel more and more the repetitions, it doesn't seem to get lighter or easier, as one might expect, but quite to the contrary, you might feel that it's getting *ever more difficult.* Alas, that's true, it's not getting easier. It's getting more difficult, because you are always going deeper. You are getting more to the bones and to the flesh of what it *really means to be incarnated in the physical.* This calls you back all the time and you feel that.

Whenever you feel that at one moment you have some kind of enlightened vision of all of existence and then suddenly you fall back into the petty details of the human's daily life – this is truly frustrating. This is the point where you need compassion, the *compassion with yourself.* Let me already state this: It is very important to realize, the moment you feel that you reverted from what is called an enlightened state back into the normal human limited state. The moment you notice that, *you are already on your way back to enlightenment,* even though it doesn't feel like that. This is compassion – being able to practice over and over again without judging yourself.

These three pillars together: true wisdom, practice, and compassion, I will call henceforth "the Eye of Suchness" or "applying the Eye of Suchness". Suchness means *beingness,* things as they are, existence as it is, pure consciousness *without any distortion.* This is beingness, suchness, *just this.* And the Eye of Suchness means: I'm aware of the things as they are. *I am aware of the things as they are.* And whatever I can see, whatever I'm aware of, well, this cannot be me.

This is the opposite to the biological eye, the eye of separation, your physical eye that is in your skull. It is an instrument of separation by its very definition. Whatever a physical sense perceives comes by way of separation. We have the external object. We have some waves or whatever, that are coming to your physical senses and then you have the reaction of the physical sense. Then you add all kinds of interpretations and memories, and then you call this a perception. This is already absolutely and totally distorted. This is the very reason why – if we are sitting here and all of you are listening to the talk – you will all have *absolutely personal* experiences of this. There are no two entities who have ever experienced the same thing. They cannot. Each and everybody is absolutely enclosed in his own world. That is the way of perception with the eyes, with the physical senses.

The Eye of Suchness, well, it's *instantly shifting into true practice*, into seeing things as they truly are, which is the true wisdom. And then you add compassion. *Seeing things as they are requires tremendous compassion*, specifically with those who are not aware of this, who are still in the game, who are trying to achieve all kind of stupid things in their daily lives, and what they do usually is, they're just creating more suffering for themselves. The moment you realize this, you want to help, but you can't. You just can't. You cannot provide wisdom like you provide a bottle of water, you just can't. Nobody was able to provide it to you, and it's a hard realization that you cannot provide it to anybody else, so you need compassion. For the others and for yourself. This is the Eye of Suchness, and I will come back quite a lot of times to this term.

Now, if you feel into this room, you might think that we are just eight humans sitting here. But this room is actually very, very full, for we are not alone. I have said already that your true self is very close, but not just your true self. With your true self came all the emanations and incarnations your true self ever had. Your past lifetimes and your future lifetimes, and even all those alien forms that you might have heard of, non-physical life forms. Even physical life forms that look kind of strange.

They might be here more or less conscious. They might be here as truly conscious visitors or they might be in their respective timeframe and they're just sensing that something is going on, something is just going on. Just as some of you have stated you just knew you had to be here. They know they have to be aware as something is going on. It might very well be that those incarnations in other lifetimes – be it in the past or in the future – they gather together in a group just like this, and they're pondering the very same question: What are the right means to see things as they are?

They might sit in a temple, a huge temple. They might sit in a church, they might be hidden somewhere in caves, because they might be prosecuted. They might sit somewhere in Atlantis.

Anywhere. They are driven by the same questions as you: "Who am I?", "Why am I here?" and "This is not the real thing, so how can I see things as they are? How can I even get out of here?"

So why do they sneak in? Because they've been made aware by your true self and by those who are helping us in this gathering. While they are aware and open to receive, they might feel when you come to an insight, when you come to the realization of true wisdom, a true understanding. If you do, then it permeates throughout your true self. It becomes available as a brightly shining potential for all of your other brothers and sisters in your true self, for all the other incarnations. They might not grasp it immediately, but it's suddenly available to them. And if they are open and aware, they can feel it and realize it also.

This is the way it works. This is the reason why sometimes, out of the blue, you just *knew* something. Maybe it was because some other incarnation of your true self had that insight, and it has spread out and suddenly was there for you. You thought it was *your* insight, but who cares in the end. It's not so important.

So, they have an eye and an ear, an inner ear, directed towards this gathering, because here we have a *huge* potential. A *huge* potential to go *very, very deep*. Just note where we are – we are in a *normal* room, we are not in a big church, not in a big pyramid, not in a big temple. You have let go of all of this, because all these great buildings were more or less just reverences to what you thought were big gods and deities and powers *outside of you*. To come close to the big thing, you have to *build* big, and then go in there and *feel* big.

Well, it might have been appropriate, but over time you've come to understand that this is just misleading. There's nothing outside, you see. So, we can just meet in a normal room in a normal city, we can talk about *anything*. There have not been too many times in human history where humans were able to talk about everything openly. The Christians have been prominent in the western world for nearly 2000 years. It was *so difficult* to have any other opinion or even to deviate just a little bit from the official dogma. Same in the eastern parts. Same *still* in many parts of the world. But here... here we can talk about things like "you are God also". Imagine that, and the others do not even look scared or weird at you, no, they share the same, say, idea, the same understanding. Maybe not yet quite the same realization, but they know the truth of it, and they're approaching it.

So here we have a very, very high potential to get very deep. To do so, the plan is to cover also new ground that we have not spoken about before, but we're trying to go there. Therefore, we have two more guests. I will introduce them briefly and they will come up later. Both will play important roles, let's say, in the background of what is going on here.

The first one is an entity that is extremely hard to put into words. The reason is – and I call her a "she" – she was *never* incarnated. She never was even in separation. Imagine that! A being that was *never in any way within separation*. Oh yes, she has heard of it, she knows of it. But she's *in no way* tarnished by it. You might say she is absolutely pure. *Absolutely pure consciousness.*

She goes by the name of Ila. I hope, none of you have ever heard of her. You have no history with her. Her name is Ila, and when she introduced herself without words but with feelings, the best Joachim came up with was "the unborn Goddess of Female Beingness". The unborn Goddess of Female Beingness and quite frankly, when Joachim came up with the word "Goddess", he wanted to throw up, because he just doesn't like all this feminine-masculine talk of the humans, no. But still, it was the best term to transport the feeling. She also goes by the name of "the Goddess of Bliss". So, these are the two ways you might feel her. It is very difficult to put her into words, because every word you use is a very crude and very raw approximation of what she really represents, so she will come here merely by the feeling and I assume, we will only speak indirectly of her.

The second guest is both a group consciousness and a group of entities. They go by the name of "Uru". Uru is a sub-branch of the family of Uriel. They're a group consciousness and they are individuals, some of them have ascended. They join us, because they are highly, highly interested and even involved in the whole process of embodied ascension, and there's a good reason for that. The reason why they are so involved in embodied ascension is because they have also been very much involved in the process of *embodiment* as such, meaning incarnating, melding consciousness and matter.

Melding consciousness and matter – this will be the hot topic of this gathering, but I have to say, we have so much on the plate that I really have to see what we can bring in into this gathering. That's why I repeat what Joachim has said in the beginning – it's very good and very wise that you have the audio recordings, for we will touch upon many topics. Many of them will come through as the words, and they are accompanied by the feelings. But it will take a while until they really settle and until you really grasp what it means in the depth. So maybe it's helpful for you to know that there is a fifth book coming up. Joachim says it will be the final book... we are not so sure about that, but there we will also highlight some topics that we will discuss here.

There are two more things I want to point in my opening speech that are so important when it comes to the practice, and these are *deconditioning* and *desensitizing*.

Deconditioning, I've already touched briefly upon, it means undoing the patterns, and this is not done quickly. It is the responsibility of the human, *he* has to do it, nobody can do it for him.

If you really want to go beyond separation, you have to *decondition* yourself. And this is done by means of true practice. Whenever you feel you're trapped or you're back into the patterns, you apply the Eye of Suchness and just move out.

Then we have desensitizing. The desensitizing is specifically of importance if you plan to survive enlightenment as an embodied enlightened being. The reason is simply that as you let go more and more and you approach more and more your natural state of pure consciousness, the human perceives this as overwhelming. It is *so intense* that the human typically shies away – never to come again, at least not in the current lifetime. The other extreme would be, well, just to go in, just to be, say... not sucked to the other side, but to follow the natural attraction of the other side and to be, in a sense, home again.

So, if you plan to stay here, it is good to desensitize yourself. We will do this in this gathering by means of the light body exercise. It is important to be really aware of these two topics. Deconditioning. Desensitizing. This is what the human can do. You see, neither is an actual doing or making! It is a "letting go" and a "getting used to" – both are passive other than you have to be aware and you have to find the time to just allow it.

So, I've already talked very much, even more than I assumed. We have already greeted, but now it's time to have a deeper greeting by doing what

I call "true encounter". To do so, I ask you to partner with a neighbor of yours. Move your chairs
such that you are sitting in front of each other and
keep your eyes closed. So please, find a partner.

*

Take on a straight position. Your back is
stretched. It's a position of *clarity*. A position of
clarity is *very* important whenever you practice
enlightenment. When you do the true practice or
when you do the light body exercise, take on a
position of clarity, of royalty, of grace. To do so,
straighten the back. One of the benefits when the
back is straight is that the breathing can go very
deep.

Breathe through your nose, let the breath come
in. Get very grounded in your physical body. By
that I mean, become aware of it. Become aware
of the *totality* of your physical body.

The easiest way to do so, is to feel your body
weight. Feel the weight of your body as it presses
against the chair and your feet rest on the floor.
Just feel, feel the pressure.

Breathe slowly through the nose. [A dog
barks.] Whatever you hear from the outside other
than this voice talking to you, just let it go. If
there's a dog barking or a car is passing by, it is
not your concern.

When you feel truly rested, relaxed in your
body, you will then open your eyes. Not yet, I will
explain some more, keep your eyes closed. But

when you're ready, you open your eyes. Usually, humans do not look into each other's eyes for more than a split second or at most a few seconds. For, as it's said, the eyes are the gateway to the soul.

So, people typically shy away from eye contact, for they feel exposed and they do not want to show everything to another person. But the truth is the other person knows mostly everything anyway [chuckles]. But by having the eye contact, by allowing the other person to connect truly with you, you also connect with yourself and with the other. Then you will see that in the end, you are not so different.

Because you have brought so many incarnations with you and so many incarnations of you are around you, weird things might happen. Weird from the perspective of the human. As you allow the soft gaze, you might see that the face of the other shifts. It might become a totally different person. A man, a woman. Somebody having a beard or long hair. You just keep the soft gaze into the eyes of the other and stay aware. You notice what's going on, you're not shocked and not surprised, just allow this to happen. There are so many of you here right now and, in a sense, they all want to greet each other, because they have known each other for a long time.

So, if you're ready, open your eyes.

*

If you feel any resistance, just let it go, continue breathing.

Even though you're having eye contact you might feel that you actually perceive with all that you are.

For some, it has been a long time since they have met.

*

It is easiest to keep this awareness while sitting. But now we're going to get up, so try not to lose this awareness even though your physical body is moving. You see, as soon as the physical body moves, you are called back into a mode of control. But the body does not need your control to move. It just does it normally, automatically, naturally. You stay aware, applying the Eye of Suchness. So just stand up and keep the same distance to your partner.

*

Now, while maintaining the Eye of Suchness, hug your partner and then move on to the next person.

*

It's interesting how much can be said without issuing a single word [audience chuckles].

Imagine you could see or meet every human on the street just as we did now. It does not require a thing other than the willingness to just be open, to meet the other, to see the other as he truly is. Why is it so difficult, one might ask, *why* is it so difficult?

If you open up, then you see that the differences between you and the other are really *only* on the surface. The way you might have experienced things, well, sure, that's different. But the very core of you is not so different at all from the others. So why not open up? Why not greet everybody with that attitude, with applying the Eye of Suchness? This doesn't mean to stare into someone who is timid, who is shying away, but just to be open and to allow others who might notice to be in contact with you. With *all* of you, not just with this little piece of flesh and bones that you carry around right now, but with *all* of you!

Imagine how life would be more joyful, easier, how much conflict would vanish immediately. Imagine Donald Trump and Kim Jong Un meeting like that. They would have a lot of fun.

So, with that we take a break.

I am Aouwa. It is a delight for me to be with you.

2. True Self – Consciousness Entity – Three in One

I am Althar, the Crystal Dragon.

Let me take some time to really witness and enjoy the beauty that is all around. You see, when consciousness opens up, when consciousness loses some of its beliefs and its tight grips, when consciousness allows itself to let go of all the small confines of the reality it thinks it is trapped in, then beauty occurs.

It is marvelous. Consciousness opens up and then there is beauty. A human can feel it. It's a relief, it is a step towards true home. Suddenly, the colors get brighter. The warmth is nicer to the body. Senses get heightened. Opening consciousness is one of the most beautiful things to witness, and this is why I, Althar, allow myself to be so often close to humans who are on their way to enlightenment.

Even if it appears to take a long *linear* time for any given entity or human to really walk the full way of enlightenment, from my perspective it is not long at all, for I observe from beyond time. So, I am happy to witness beauty over and over again in so many different variants.

You've heard Aouwa talking in the first session about those three levels: the absolute, the relative, and the in-between. The „three in one", sometimes called the Trinity. The Trinity is something that is often spoken of. It occurs in many religions for there have been of course many insights into true reality, and then those insights have been transferred and transformed into concepts and notions and expressions. But the Trinity or the threefoldness of mostly everything exists in many, many religions.

And it is a truth! Here, we say simply the level of the true self, the level of the human, and the in-between. Trinity is something that is natural. You might say, only with the occurrence of separation did Trinity come into play, because without separation there is no relative and there is no in-between, there is just pure consciousness.

We are here in a setup where we are beyond time, and this gives us and you the opportunity to *immediately* realize your own Trinity. There is no big effort necessary to get there. It is not just a choice, but it is also not much more than a choice. It is *absolutely* possible.

I say we are beyond time to emphasize for each and every one of you sitting here, that your personal life you've undergone up to this point is not really of importance. In a sense, you can just let go of it. The next time you enter this room, leave your personal life somewhere outside and come here as consciousness that experiences separation. What you've done up to this point is really of no importance. This means that in order to experience and realize the Trinity, the three in one, there are no requirements or prerequisites. You do not have to have thousands of years of practice of something. You do not need to be somewhat smart or intelligent. You do not need any specific characteristics other than the boldness to just open up and to let go.

Here in this protected environment, in this moment out of your linear time you, can experience Trinity to its fullest, and you do not have to think a millisecond about what comes after you leave this workshop in few days. Then, it might be that the experiences you have had here might get a bit foggy. They are typically condensed and get smaller. They become memories. But there is something that will stay with you – a remembrance, a knowingness, and maybe even the ability to instantly switch into the Trinity, into the Eye of Suchness.

To realize the Trinity, you need the three "ingredients" that are apparently separated. And we will bring all of them together right now. So, let's have a nice trip with some nice music and we will start with the body.

[Music plays]

I want you all to really get comfortable and relax. What we are going to do is in no way difficult, it is *natural*. It is your *true home*. Starting with the body, take on a posture of clarity. Allow your back to straighten so you can breathe deeply.

Allow your belly to move with the breath coming in, going out.

Separation is full of paradoxes, full of paradoxes, and of strange things. But once you are aware of these mechanics and strange things, you can use them for your benefit. Typically, you think that the mind influences the body. When you get agitated or emotional, the body follows, it gets crisp, or stressed. But it also works the other way around. When the body is taking on a position of clarity and is doing the deep breathing, then the *mind will follow.* The emotions will calm down.

You should be very aware of that. This is the easiest and most straightforward thing that you could do at any time in your human life. Become aware of your body. The body is always here in the now moment. Your breath is always here. So, if you are stressed, if you feel distracted, just step back. Become aware of the body and with that apply the Eye of Suchness.

Just follow the breath, feel it.

Allow the body to relax. Allow all the tension in your muscles to just dissolve. In a position of clarity, when you're sitting upright, or standing upright, you need very little muscle power to keep that posture. If you are upright, you are in balance. If your head is upright and not dangling down as if you were looking on your smartphone, then you do not need any muscles of your neck to stabilize the head. So, you can completely relax.

Humans think that their consciousness is somehow *within* them, in their brain. But nothing, nothing, nothing can be more wrong. From my perspective, the human is typically very scattered, very scattered.

You might remember when you were a kid, when you were holding a balloon filled with hot air or gas. It was floating upward, and you held some thread to keep the balloon with you. Human consciousness is very much like that. You have, say, bubbles or balloons of your consciousness that are spread out into the past, into the future, and even into the now moment, to the left, and to the right. You are holding on to them. You are constantly monitoring the past. For this is where you made your decisions that led you to the now moment, and this is what you project into the future.

Right now, you might have parts and pieces of you that are, say, with your parents, your kids, your pets or your plants, taking care of them, somehow being with them, somehow monitoring them. Some part of you is here sitting in this chair. Now I want you to bring back all these small balloons of consciousness that are out there swirling and dancing and watching and observing. Bring them back into this now moment. You might imagine them to come to join with the consciousness that is in and around your physical body.

If you are engaged in a, say, sophisticated project, so much consciousness is bound to that project somewhere out there, and it stays there. Bring it back. Think of the balloon. You pull the string and the balloon is slowly coming to you. Take some time to just collect whatever comes to your mind. Whatever you think you have to monitor.

Pull in the future. Whatever you might expect from the future, be very honest with you, is most often surrounded by fear, because so often you want certain things *not* to happen. Pull it in. Pull it in.

If you have kids, a part of you is always with them, always sensing them somehow, monitoring, observing, wanting to take care. Bring that part in. Pull in the string of the balloon.

As you do that, you might feel a certain relaxation within you. You are relieved. You're getting *fuller*.

Pull in those strings from the past. Bring them in. Remembrances of where you have come from, where you have grown up. Parts and pieces of you have spread across your timeline. They cannot let go of certain incidents. But here and now, in this now moment, you can just bring them home to you. Gently pull in those balloons, obtaining your consciousness.

Whenever you feel stress in your daily life, check yourself. Are there parts and pieces of you out there, somewhere? Even trying to interfere there, to control?

Or maybe they are out there for problem solving, I mean *real* problem solving, like analyzing a scientific equation. Then you may notice that there are parts and pieces of you out there constantly working on it.

Bring it home to relax.

While breathing in, bring all of the consciousness to you, all of those balloons. Breathe through *all* of your skin, not just through the nose. Imagine that each pore of your skin contains a thread that is connected to a consciousness bubble of yours that is somewhere out there. Just breathe them in.

Ah, you might notice the clarity that comes in, the ease. You're not responsible for everything, you are not. Being fully present in your body, being relaxed, being in clarity – this is "one in one". You have to start there, always, always, always. If you cannot be in clarity and presence within your body, realizing the trinity remains elusive. It will remain just another concept floating out there.

So, now that you are more present, more clear in your body, let's leave the body behind and we journey, we journey outward. Your biological body is fully capable of sustaining itself. It doesn't need your help, so you can just leave it here. We float, we float outward. So, follow me, we go up, straight through the ceiling. We travel as consciousness, we float higher and higher. Like in Google Earth, when you are zooming out. You've zoomed into a location and then you zoom out. Here, in the Cascais, zooming out, you suddenly see the whole village, the town, you go further up and further up. You see the ocean, the Atlantic, the huge ocean.

Further and further. The Earth becomes smaller.

Have a look at the Earth, isn't she beautiful?

Isn't it astonishing how things get simple and beautiful if you just move away a little bit? Here, from this perspective the problems of the human are of not so big importance. You can marvel at the Earth.

But now we turn around. Even if you have no body, you most often keep a sense of direction. So, move in the direction away from the sun. Now the sun is behind you, we move further and further. Feel that, float gently. The further we get away from planet Earth, the further we get away from being incarnated, being in flesh, being tied to matter.

Now we are so far away that the Earth has become a dot. She's not even visible anymore. But look out at the firmament. There are *so many* stars all around – billions and billions of stars. So much light. So much light. Look at all those stars. Embrace them.

One of those stars, a sun, is making itself stand out just for you – it's your personal sun. Everybody has its own. Just find that sun and float there. Get closer and closer.

Oh, that sun is *huge*. Earth is huge compared to a human, but this sun is so much *grander*, so much *larger*. It emanates so much energy, so much heat, so much light, it is so huge. The closer you get, the more you let go of all of your human concepts, human notions of time and space, of wants and needs, of patterns. Nothing, nothing,

nothing of this plays any role out here – you are just here, approaching that sun. *Your* sun, a gigantic sun.

It is hot, not just a few degrees, but millions and millions of degrees. As you are getting closer and closer to that sun, you notice that you cannot really make out a surface of this sun. You cannot really say where the sun begins or ends. The sun has no surface, no skin.

You go deeper into it, you enter it. It doesn't hurt, it doesn't hurt a bit. You feel the heat, not as burning, but as a relaxation. You might even hear things cracking, notions and concepts that you held tightly on to, like wood in a fire.

Isn't it interesting, you are here without any body, but still you have notions and patterns and conditionings of which you are not so much aware, but they drop away.

Even though the sun is huge, you can go right into the center of it. Distance is of no importance to us.

As you are in the center of the sun now, *grow*, get larger. *Become the whole sun*, radiate out. You are not a small human within a sun, no-no. Now you become that sun, radiating, shining, without agenda. It's just your nature to bring your light forth, to let it shine, to let it radiate.

Feel that for a moment – you are shining in all directions. Now, while you are one with the sun, see all the other seven suns that have been chosen by those traveling with you. They are also shining their light. And when you perceive *their* light, you can feel that their light is not so much different from your light.

Their light extends outward from what can be called the center of their sun, but it extends outward and touches you. Now, where does your sun end and the other sun begin? They intermingle. There is no true separation, yet they are, in a sense, still unique. They are their own suns.

Let's arrange our suns in a circle. Like your humans are sitting in this room on planet Earth in a circle. Let's arrange the suns in a huge, huge circle.

Send some light to planet Earth and to this room.

Now, let's do an experiment, let's turn off the light! Let your sun become darker and darker, ever darker. Turn off the light.

Now, there is darkness – *nothing* to perceive, nothing to perceive. You see, some humans are very visual, whenever you say a word – they have pictures or a whole film, and some are not visual at all. They have just the words and they complain: "Oh, I didn't see or didn't feel anything, it was weird to me." But maybe, just maybe, this is an advantage. Because in the end, whatever you perceive, you *have* to let go. Whatever you can see *cannot be you.*

It is perception that creates reality in separation.

Seeing light is a choice and it binds you to the worlds of separation. Interesting worlds, but not the true reality.

Whatever you perceive, cannot be you. Perception is creation in the world of separation.

Let's turn on the light again. Let's continue dissolving illusions with illusions.

Ah, the universe is back. There's planet Earth. Even though we are far away, as a grand sun that we are, we can see planet Earth very clearly, and we can even see the group of people sitting here in Cascais.

The human likes to equate his true self with something like a sun – a grand thing, radiating, shining, without agenda, untouched by anything, free.

So, let's take this sun as a symbol for your true self. Let's observe from the perspective of your true self the human that is sitting in his chair in Cascais. As you are a good true self you can, of course, see beyond the now moment – you can see into the past, you can see into the future, you can see your whole timeline.

Observe that human and take note of how much energy your human incarnation uses each day for his or her biology. *Every day.* To maintain the biology, to earn money so you can buy food. Then, buying the food, preparing the food, eating the food, doing the dishes, disposing the rest of the food. *Every day.* Cleaning the body. So much activity simply to maintain the biology. See it on the timeline, you might even color the timeline, color in red the time your human spends for maintaining its human body, including health and trying to have a fit body. So much activity. All that activity is reinforcing your belief of being a human, of being incarnated.

At the same time, you have an emotional body. A human has, what I call, false identities. "False" simply, because *every* identity is false unless you take it on as an act. Each identity is a false identity, and the human has plenty of them. Yes, you have integrated or you became aware of many of them, but some are still there in one way or the other.

They want attention, they want validation. They never agree on anything, not amongst each other, not with your physical body. They have opinions on everything, judgments. Whatever they perceive while having access to perception, they relate it to what they think they are. Is it validated or is it rejected? The perception becomes good or bad in the eye of that false identity. This is going on constantly. Even while you're cooking food, you have the voices: "Don't eat this, don't eat that", "Chocolate cookie is good", "Ah, no, too many calories" – this is always going on, constantly. The emotional body is very seldomly in harmony with the physical body.

Then you have the mental body. The very same goes on here, just in a different strata, you might say. The mental body might work on true challenges, like scientific problems that it wants to explore, but most often what the mental body does is spinning the same old wheels, thinking the same old thoughts, most often being occupied by the emotional body.

What is it that you really need to think of in your daily life? There's not so much new happening, so why all this commotion in the mental?

As a true self you can see all of this and say: "Woah! Might be good to send some help…" Now, I call myself Althar, the Crystal Dragon. I've introduced myself as the dragon of compassion. I've also said, I am a bridge in consciousness. I am all of that. So, maybe it would be good for you to have something similar, made of your true self. Thus, as a true self, *emanate* a consciousness being. It might be a dragon, it might be anything that you relate to. Emanate something, like a dragon.

You might see it and picture it in front of you. If you don't see it, your life becomes easier – you won't have so much trouble to let go of it. Anyway, bring it forth. It is *you*! It will move towards planet Earth.

So, let's do that. Let's ride that dragon or whatever you have chosen. We soar back to Earth. The sun, the true self, remains here. Let your consciousness being soar back to planet Earth. Just as we have come, we get closer and closer to Earth.

The Earth becomes bigger, you see the ocean, you see the land, the city, the house. Let's stop right at the ceiling. We are hovering at the ceiling.

Feel that. Your consciousness being is there, feeling the energies.

Now, just as we have greeted this morning with the true encounter, human to human, eye to eye, let those consciousness beings greet each other.

Even though you might think they are very fresh, just birthed, this is not really the case. They come from your true self, and as such they have access to all of your true self. *They know it all*, so to speak. So, they are as ancient as your true self is. They are beyond time. Just birthed and already ancient. Cool stuff, huh?

So, greet them.

You see, what you are doing as a human, is not something you do alone, truly not, and this is a blessing. You have helpers on so many levels. You might not be aware of them, for they do not interfere. But believe me, they are helping, they are assisting, they do whatever they can to prepare the grounds for you without interfering. They cannot do it for you, of course, but they are there in the moment you ask for companionship.

So, now, let your consciousness being descend down, place it directly in front of you, like we have sat in the morning with your human partner. But now your partner is your consciousness being. It is looking straight into your eyes, assuming that your consciousness being has eyes. If not, just create some.

Allow that consciousness being... I will call it a dragon, if you have something else – just replace it internally. Let that dragon see into your eyes and you into the eyes of the dragon.

In the exercise this morning, you were doing it more or less from the human perspective. Opening up, as good as you could. Still hiding this and that, not being very confident with yourself, although it felt good.

There are things within yourself that you do not want to see, and you have suppressed them so strongly that you even cannot see them. But the consciousness being, your dragon, *is* of your true self. *It knows it all and it can see it.*

So, there's no need to hide, or to be timid, or to shy away. It knows it all anyway. More than you do, more than you do. The dragon just whispers to you: "It is okay, it is okay. This is all a dream, and whatever you did in your dream *is not real*. There is no need for a happy ending. You can just let go, just accept."

See into the eyes of your dragon and the dragon shows you *all* that you are within.

To make this even easier, just let your consciousness from the human float into the dragon. Switch the perspective.

The physical human being sits in the chair, but your consciousness goes into your dragon and sees through the dragon's eyes into itself, into all that the human does not want to see. All of your unresolved issues, fears, strong wants and desires, traumas, shame.

Seen from the perspective of the dragon, being beyond time, being beyond separation, *you see the things as they truly are*. And the truth is, well, in a sense, *nothing has ever happened*. Therefore, there's no need to carry it with you, to make it real by holding onto it.

That is the wisdom of the dragon.

You can radiate it without any words as the *full acceptance* of all that you are, of all that you know that you are, and of all that you have suppressed.

Feel that, feel the acceptance.

Now let the dragon come closer. It embraces you, it is within you and all around you. Now you and the dragon, in a sense, become one. You are the physical, the dragon is the mystery. It is there with you, without a doubt. You can feel it. You have the wisdom, the acceptance, the compassion, the timelessness of the dragon. It is all around you, and it feels so good.

Imagine sparkling water. It's a clear liquid, but somehow there is gas in it, and it comes up as bubbles. Also, the human consciousness that is incarnated, has so many invisible bubbles of attachments, patterns, judgments. They are hidden in the consciousness, just like the gas in sparkling water, but with the presence of the dragon, they become bubbles and float upward and dissolve.

The dragon shines a bright light on everything that is hidden within you. And the dragon is *calm*. It knows, it's okay, no need to panic, it's a dream.

Now, having the physical and the mystery, the dragon, we have the "two in one". Feel that again for a moment. A kind of melding of the dragon with you, with what you think you are.

Silently, without moving your arms, you might spread your wings, just spread them and feel the grandiosity of all that you are in this very moment. *Nothing* can harm you, you know that. Nothing can harm you. Spreading your wings is *such* a symbol.

Now let's continue, let's bring in true self. It is out there as a sun, remember? Apparently far, far away. So, let's take that symbol of a sun and let it get closer, closer and closer.

Somehow the size changes as the sun approaches you. The size becomes like that of an orange – very handy. Feel how it comes closer as a radiant ball of light. It comes closer and closer and stops some 30-40 cm above your head. Feel that, *feel* that!

You as a human, one with your dragon, with the mystery, the in-between. Your true self is just above you. Oh, what a beauty! Now, if you so choose, allow your true self, this light, to slowly, slowly come down, through your skull, right into your heart. Slowly, slowly. As it does, you might feel a sensual... even sexual stimulation. Do not get distracted by that, just observe it.

Allow the true self to come into you, into your heart.

Now let this true self of you, this sun within you, get a bit larger and larger, until it embraces you with your dragon, the dragon with the wings spread. And then, when you have that size of your true self, hold that image and feel. *Take note* of that feeling. A feeling of completion.

Now the true self becomes larger and larger. It obtains the size of the sun we've visited, but it gets even larger and larger. Can you feel that? You're still in the midst of it. As a human, as a dragon. *There is no difference.* You fill the whole true self just as you filled the whole sun. This sun, your true self, gets larger and larger.

Let it fill *all of the universe!* Don't be humble. Allow that to happen. Distance is not a problem for true self.

Where does true self begin and where does it end? Where is the inside and where is the outside?

This is the "three in one", the Trinity.

Here we are in this timeless moment. Timeless, beyond your linear timescale. You see, you just get into this office space you are sitting in right now, take a trip, and you are there – what you have searched for eons, you can now experience. Why? Because you're ready. Because you allow it. Because you had enough of the standstill, enough of the repetition of always the same things. That's why! You've asked for it and so it is.

Take note of that feeling. Seen from this grand perspective, is there any problem you have? I mean, really, *really?*

Is there anything missing in this very moment?

This is what I call the "expanding perfection" – nothing is missing.

Allow yourself to take on the big perspective – this is the Eye of Suchness. It is a grand perspective. It is beyond perception. It is the awareness of things as they truly are.

The Eye of Suchness is always with you, always available to you. In essence, choosing it is the only true power you have as a human. Do you want to experience through the Eye of Suchness or do you want to enforce and solidify separation by perceiving things with the eye of separation? *That is the choice* you have to make. And you have to make it *instant by instant, over and over again.*

As long as you are in the human body, conditioned to be a human – *this* is the choice you have to make *over and over again*, until at some point, there is no choice left. Because it is your natural state that you finally, finally come back to.

All the separation would be so easy to leave if we now could just close the session and your expanded consciousness remained. But I predict that it tends to go back to your human mode as soon as you move, as soon as you talk, as soon as you go out to eat, as soon as you discuss what you've experienced. And slowly, slowly you fall back into your human mode. Yes, a bit expanded, a deep memory, a deep experience with you. But there are some forces within you that call you back to the flesh and to the bones. This is what we will dive into in the sessions to come.

So, if possible, just maintain this openness, this state. There's nothing in the universe that forces you to go back into human mode – although it is difficult to stay expanded, I admit that.

For me, Althar, it was a grandiose spectacle to witness you in this session, and believe me, I was not the only one to witness – we had plenty of spectators. They're in awe of what you're doing, for so many cannot imagine what it means to fully, fully forget about your true self. What it means not to know who you are. What it means to be in separation and then trying to somehow create a way back. *They cannot imagine this*, but they observe. There is a deep reason why you do this – you are really appreciated and admired for doing so.

With that, I wish you a good lunch break, feed yourselves. Enjoy the eating, and we will meet in the afternoon for the next session.

I am Althar, the Crystal Dragon.

3. Space – Microcosm – Macrocosm

I am Althar, the Crystal Dragon!

I am really happy to be back with you. I wished we could do all this without using words, but sometimes words are just necessary. But I promise you, there will come the time when you will be able to convey what we have experienced here to people who approach you, even without words. They will be able to contact you, to meld with you, and to hook on to your experiences. Then, they can experience so much more easily the very same within themselves. What we are doing here is breaking the ice for all the rest to come. We will use words, we will use, say, guided meditations, we will use all kinds of illusions to loosen you up.

Now, the human realm is defined by three core intentions. First, time. Second is space, and then we have the veiling. Veiling of mostly every portion and level of your consciousness that you are aware of. What remains is an entity that is so immersed in the physical body, bound to a timeline, crawling along it, sometimes dancing along it. The veiling makes sure that this entity does not know who it really is. It has no real remembrance or association of where it comes from, so it's lost in a very dense environment. Yet, all of us have chosen this environment for a very good purpose. The purpose was, as you might recall, to overcome this standstill.

Standstill meaning the realization that whatever happens in separation is based on repetition.

Everything, in a sense, is already there, you are always reliving the same plots, the same storylines, the same experiences. Yes, you get older, yes, the others change a little bit, even the fashion might change, but in the end, you always play out the very same storylines. The moment you realize this, you are *shocked*, hopefully, and you want to get out. At some point, you have just enough of running through the various experiences of separation and you just want to know: *How can I get out?*

The agreement, the idea, was to try to get your way out by means of incarnating in physical reality. Tomorrow, we will speak more about how this incarnating took place and why it was so important. Today, we will focus on one of those core intentions that you are locked into – and this is *space*.

Imagine a being that is not bound to space and which has no physical body. A being without a physical body. Can you imagine what that means? There is no pain! Such an entity *knows no pain*. If there is no pain and if there's no physical death, then whatever you do has, in a sense, no real consequences as you know it, as a human. So, whatever you do without a physical body might be interesting, but at the same time it appears to be somehow pointless. There are no morals. What would be the point of morals if you can do whatever you want, and nobody is really getting harmed?

So, if you think of the standstill, what it means to be in the non-physical, it is even more apparent and even clearer that it is so difficult to overcome it there. But here in the physical, in the very slow-motion density where you believe you have cause and effect, and where you can see what action you initiate has as a consequence, here you can suddenly understand what this is all about. Down here, in the density of the physical, you can understand that something like separation even exists. The very notion of separation becomes clear to you, because everything you experience is in so damned slow-motion for you. However, once you realize this, doesn't mean that it's easy to get out.

So, space is one of the core intents that was agreed upon to create the human experience. It is kind of your contract. You want to come here for the experience? Then you have to agree to space, otherwise you could not have a joint experience. Same for time. Same for veiling.

In order to get out, to free yourself from the core intentions, we will do some "consciousness stretching". We want to make each and everyone of you aware that you are *absolutely* flexible when it comes to space and to time. You are free, and the easiest way to do it is by means of exercising, going in and out into the micro and macro cosmos. This is precisely what we are going to do now.

Once again, I will play some music that will guide us.

[Music plays]

Allow yourself to really feel what I am trying to convey beyond all of my words. It is important. Space is one of the core characteristics of your physical existence. Space is one of those rubber bands that always, always pulls you back into the human identity, into the human experience, even though you might have experienced Trinity just an hour ago. Space is one of those rubber bands.

I have said this morning that whenever you are about to do an exercise, we suggest here, you start with your physical body. Take on a clear posture, and it should be also a posture of joy, of grace even, for what we are doing here is of the highest a human can do. The *highest* a human can do! A human that stretches out to reach into the divine – *this* is what we are about to do. It is not a well-being exercise, it is not a "feeling good" thing – it is the *highest* a human can do, so it's appropriate to take on the posture of clarity, the posture of grace, the posture of royalty, the posture of the divine human that you are going to become.

So, straighten your back. Make sure you relax all the tensions in your muscles, your shoulders, in your legs, in your hands.

Observe how the breath is coming into your nose. Do not breathe actively. Do not try to do anything. Just allow the breath to enter your nose, to fill your entire body, and then allow it to go out again with the breathing out.

As you allow the breathing in a clear posture, your mind settles, becomes quiet and calm. It adapts.

This is so easy. In the end, everything is *so* easy. Let the breath come and go. The physical body is coming to clarity. It might even be tired after the lunch break, which is a good thing. Let it sleep, let the body just fall asleep. Your body might sleep, and you can be *totally* clear.

Now, you know that consciousness is beyond space just as I, Althar am beyond space. I can take on any form and any size, and so can you.

So now, please let your consciousness... I wouldn't say shrink down, but let your consciousness focus on a small spot below your nose, just above your upper lip. Just feel that area. It is a highly sensitive area.

As you breathe calmly through your nose, feel the air touching this area.

Just feel this region, how the air enters your nose, comes back, gently touching a part of your upper lip. You know, Buddha became enlightened when doing exactly this exercise. He had let go of everything, he was just aware of the breath coming in and going out and suddenly everything opened up. Everything opened up to him. He had already stopped searching, had stopped the ascetic practices and just sat down, relaxed in an upright position. And he simply was with his breathing.

So, feel the breath in that area of the upper lip. There are tiny, tiny hairs. You might even see them or visualize them as they move when the breath is going in and out.

You are tiny and your body is large, isn't that interesting? It feels like you, who have been the whole universe just an hour ago, is now completely present on a tiny spot on your upper lip, looking into this huge face of yours.

But consciousness is beyond size. There's no potency assigned to consciousness of a given size or extension. Consciousness remains the same no matter how you choose to perceive it.

Now, allow your consciousness to further shrink, to focus even more, and choose a *single cell* on your upper lip. Then just glide into that cell.

Allow yourself to perceive on that level, perceive within a cell.

What a different world. It's like jumping into an ocean and everything is suddenly full of fish. Outside there was just sand, sun, and the surface of the water. Your cell is full of liquids. It is truly three-dimensional. It is like a whole city in itself. There is a lot of commotion. All kinds of factories producing all kinds of chemicals, transmuting energies.

Be there, just observe. A tiny cell, a single cell of your body.

There are molecules which have propellers at their end. Truly, true story. They transport other molecules, from left to right, up, down. No human has a clue how this works, who is driving all this action. That's totally unknown to the human. They just describe it. There is this, there is that, there are some chemicals, and that's it. Each cell is a city on its own, full of life. Full of life and *wanting to live*, wanting to sustain itself.

Now as you glide around in your cell, you approach the nucleus of the cell. Just go in there. Just go into the nucleus. What you see are those grand, grand DNA molecules. So many, so complex. They are wound up. If you would stretch a single DNA molecule, if it is stretched out, it would have a length of 1 meter and 80 centimeters. Can you imagine that? This is all just wound around itself and placed inside the single cell. Not just one molecule, but plenty of them. Be there, feel the action. The DNA plays a very important role when it comes to incarnating.

Choose a DNA molecule and glide along it. Become ever tinier. Glide along it. It's like a spiral stairway. Just glide along it.

The DNA is like a stream of information. So many patterns are anchored here. Biological patterns, even emotional patterns. Just continue gliding along. DNA even has non-physical strands to it. Unseen to the human eye, but very active. Glide along. This molecule is very, very long and you are very, very tiny.

Feel the world from the perspective of a DNA molecule. There's communication going on between the chemicals that are flowing in and out.

Now make a stop. Choose an atom, an atom of your liking. Just as you have chosen a sun in the morning, now choose an atom. Feel into that atom. As we get tinier and tinier, the environment gets more and more fuzzy. What is an electron, what is an atom? There's a hull, they call it a cloud. They say that the electrons are moving and swirling. The electrons, in a sense, do not really exist. They are all around. They are everywhere and in a certain position they can be measured to an extent, but in the end it all comes down to probabilities.

So, there's a cloud, a potential of electrons being there, surrounding the nucleus of the atom. Feel that, the commotion, the energy we have here.

Once again, an atom in itself is comparatively *huge*, so huge. If you place a grain of rice in the middle of a soccer field, then the electrons will be the outer ranks of the stadium that is built around that soccer field. In-between, what is in-between? There is space. How do they connect? Why are they together? The electron and the nucleus.

So, dive into this cloud of the electrons. Come closer to the nucleus. Just as we have gone closer from the outer space to Earth in the morning. Approach the nucleus. Feel the nucleus.

The nucleus is like spheres, small balls of protons and neutrons. *And they cling together!* They cling together.

What is a proton or a neutron? Dive into it. Dive into it. The deeper you go, the fuzzier it gets. Is there even a "deeper"? The scientists are not clear what is on that level. They have many theories: abstract forces, strings, energetic configurations, even geometries. They are not yet clear. It's hard to observe what's going on there. But could it be that the details create themselves when they're needed?

So here we are in the very depths of what is known as physical matter. Wherever you look you see not so much. We are on the level of forces that cannot be touched, cannot be seen. But when we go up a little bit from here to the protons and neutrons – they can be measured and visualized. They seem to exist.

Now feel into the energy that is present on this level. You know what happens if you tear apart the nucleus of an atom. Do this with a few atoms at the same time and you'll have an atomic bomb, a nuclear bomb. Tear them apart and – boom! – a whole city suddenly vanishes. All life is extinguished. High, high energies are set free. Everything is immediately burned. Puffff! Bodies are instantly pulverized. Such are the energies on this level. Feel that for a moment. You might even *embrace* the nucleus. Embrace it, feel it. Just like the dragon engulfed you and was all around you and within you in the morning – do the very same with the nucleus of the atom.

Isn't matter a strange thing? Isn't space a strange thing?

Now, let's go backward. From this nucleus zoom outwards, see the whole atom again. Then the DNA, and the cell from within. Then be once again on your upper lip.

There's an interesting phenomenon with consciousness: If it has gone one way once, it becomes much easier to go the way again and again. So, let's just dive back, let's just dive back from the upper lip, again into the cell, the nucleus of cell, glide along a DNA molecule, stop at an atom. Dive deep into the nucleus, and even deeper to the abstract forces. Be there.

Now let's add a rhythm to it. When you breathe, in you go all the way back to your upper lip. When you breathe out, you go all the way into the very center of an atom.

It's getting fluid, you see, it's *so* flexible. Once you get used to this, consciousness gets flexible. That's why I call this "consciousness stretching" or "belief system stretching". Space is not fixed. Your appearance within space is not fixed!

With breathing out, go inwards. Then all the way back.

In and out.

We've just visited one single cell, but your whole body consists of approximately 10^{14} cells.

This is a one followed by 14 zeroes. Quite a number.

Go in again, into this single cell. Down to the nucleus, the atom, the abstract forces.

If you are so bold, you might imagine how you do this simultaneously with *all of your cells*. Do not ask *how* you do it, *just do it* – you are flexible.

Say hello to each and every cell and atom that you encounter. This is a very different way to feel your body, isn't it? Just a shift of perspective.

A final trip. Go deep within and then come back to your normal body size, to the awareness of your physical body as you are used to.

Now, we go in the other direction. As we've done this already in the morning, we are now used to it and we can go *immediately* to the sun. Send your consciousness to the sun, to the sun that is responsible for Earth.

We are there immediately. See the Earth from here. Feel all the humans. Isn't it interesting that there are about 7 billion humans on Earth. 7 billion is a 7 with 9 zeros. But your body consists of "1 and 14 zeroes" cells. Anyway, see the humans from here, *feel* them. Those few billion humans are nothing against the cells of yours.

Now, go further into the cosmos, away from the sun. Earth vanishes, even the sun gets smaller. We zoom out more and more and more. Oh, there's the Milky Way, suddenly. Unseen before, but now from the outside, you can see it. What is the Milky Way? Billions and billions of stars, but the Milky Way is tiny compared to the rest that you have in your cosmos.

Go further away from the Milky Way. Zoom out even more. You get all kinds of gigantic cosmic formations. Spirals, fogs. Billions and billions of them. Lightyears over lightyears in extension, but we can go there quite easily. We are getting larger and larger. All the galaxies become like tiny points, the size of an atom.

Now, let's reverse the direction. Slowly we get towards Earth. We travel. Suddenly, the Milky Way appears. A moment ago, it was a point, but now it's getting larger and larger, and we see it consists of billions and billions of stars. Within those billions of stars there's our sun. We greet the sun, "Hello, sun!" We continue moving towards Earth, to your human body, sitting here. Take a pause, a breath.

Then we go out again. But now we double the speed. Are you ready? We zoom out again. Sun, Milky Way, galaxies. The whole universe. Can you feel that?

Now, let's get bold. *Let's go beyond the universe.* Consciousness is flexible, you see.

You might ask, "How can I do *that?* How can I go beyond the universe? There is a limited amount of space within the universe. How can I get beyond?"

But I say, "*Just* go beyond. Shift your perspective. *Get grand!*"

Suddenly, you see the universe as if it was a bubble, like a balloon filled with all the stars and Milky Ways, and Earth, and atoms. *So many* of them! But as you look around, you see so many of those balloon-like universes. *So many!*

We zoom out even further. We zoom out, and as if by accident, you see the universes are arranged. Just like the stars are arranged into galaxies and Milky Ways, so are the universes. Wherever you go, you create the details. This is true for the tiniest, tiniest of scales and for the largest of scales. Consciousness in separation is not blank, it creates, it fills its perception with something. See all these universes.

Now we go back. Thanks God, you know exactly what universe you have to dive into. It stands out. So, choose the universe in which you are in right now. You come from the outer edges, wherever that would be, back to the Milky Way, the sun, Earth and to your body. But you don't stop there! You continue into the micro cosmos. Into a cell, the nucleus of the cell, a strand of DNA, an atom, protons, neutrons, abstract forces. Stay there. Stay there and *stretch out*. Feel what you've seen just a moment before. A universe of universes. Feel both at the same time. The macro cosmos, the micro cosmos. You might say we go full spectrum. The ultimate stretching that you could do. Linear minds cannot grasp this. It says, "How can I perceive on all those scales simultaneously?" but you can.

Now I ask you this: Where does all of this take place? *How much space does space occupy within consciousness?*

Now that you span the whole spectrum, allow yourself to be very flexible. Zoom in and out, again, with each breath.

Breathing in – you go the edges of all the universes. Breathing out – you go back to the tiniest and tiniest of atoms and subatomic particles and whatever is there.

Can you feel *why a core intention is required?* Not only to bow to space, but also for fixing a certain scale on which you want to experience. If there is another entity and it decides to go on the microscale and you go on the macroscale, how could you ever share experiences? You just can't.

The same goes for time, the time scale you are operating in. You have to have *core* intentions in order to be able to share with other entities. And when it comes to the human incarnation, it is also important that you *forget* that you have these core intentions.

*

Now, go back to the micro level. Feel once again into the nucleus of an atom.

Imagine what it means for consciousness to incarnate. You see, consciousness and physical matter do not really fit together. Consciousness is so flexible. Physical matter appears to be so rigid.

So, *how* do they come together? What is it that makes you believe you are human?

Feel into this as you glide along various atoms of your physical body. Stroll around as consciousness. You might even remember the Trinity you've realized this morning. So, why not shift to the Eye of Suchness? And just flow along all these atoms that somehow make you believe you are bound to the physical body. Do it gently.

*

You are *not* your physical body. You are *not* your emotions. You are *not* your thoughts. You are consciousness in experience, in separation.

You are not bound to any space or scale. But granted, it appears to be kind of a mind thing what we're doing here. Maybe it is *just* imagination, not yet real.

We are about to loosen the connection of consciousness to the physical, and you might say, *here* is the point where it *gets real,* because *here* is something that is called death, and *the fear of death.* On the other levels, on the emotional level, mental level, even the spiritual level, it is not that risky. You might change your beliefs or attitudes, you might experience an easier life. If it works, it's good, if not – it's not threatening. You can live with difficulties up to a point. But *here* we go so deep that we even attempt to loosen the connection between consciousness and matter. You will have reactions on this very level.

As a preparation for tomorrow, reflect a bit on the following: If you, as consciousness, wanted to incarnate into physical matter, which just does not mix together very well, what would you do? *How* would *you* approach it?

Sail along the atoms with the consciousness of Trinity. See them, they are active, and in a way, they are also sleeping, aren't they?

I have another... call it homework. You felt the Trinity today, your true self, your human consciousness, and the mystery in-between. You might want to find a name for you. Maybe you have one already, for your true self. A resonance. Feel into that. It's not even necessary that this name could be spoken. Maybe you'll find a representation in your written characters that matches it somehow, like Aouwa – that's when you put it in a word, but that's not at all the vibration that's going on behind it. Same for you. Find the vibration of you. It is there, feel it, no need to pronounce it. It can even come with a light or sound or feelings – it's totally up to you.

Let's go one more time to the macro level with your Trinity consciousness, let's sail outwards. Slowly, gently. Seeing all the cells and the atoms of your body – doesn't it look like a galaxy in itself? A huge formation.

Then go out into the cosmos. All the stars. To the very edge of the cosmos and beyond to see just the same repeating patterns. Wherever you go consciousness *is* already.

That's why it is said, *consciousness has never moved.*

The only thing that moves is your focus in separation.

Consciousness is a wonderful thing. Look, what even a limited consciousness can bring forth. Consciousness bound to separation. *Unbelievable* structures, mechanisms, experiences. All based on a, oh, hard to say… *impossible* thought.

How can the unnatural exist? It can't, other than in a dream.

But here we are within that dream, and we are dismantling it. We're doing it by seeing its very building blocks, by making it simpler and simpler and simpler, until we come to the one and only thing that creates it all – it's the belief in separation.

Isn't that beautiful? As you are pondering this you might feel Ila. She is with us all the time. In a sense, she's waiting to greet you home again.

By the way, did you encounter your true self on the way? Was it somewhere out there? Has it a place in space?

For today, I will say goodbye, but I leave you with the music and the feeling of being beyond *any* scale. So, pause for a while, remain sitting, feel into yourself, into the vibration of your true self. Once again feel what it means that there's physical matter and there is consciousness that wants to embody in it. *What a strange idea!*

I am Althar and I'm with you on this journey *on* all scales and *with* my scales on my non-existing skin that are shining brightly right now.

I see you tomorrow.

4. Time – Now-spheres – Threads of Time

Joachim: You might see the lyrics of the music that I'll play next as a dragon talking to you. As the lyrics are in German, here is a translation:

To ashes, to dust
Taken away from the light
But not just yet
Miracles wait until the end

Ocean of time
Eternal law
To ashes, to dust
But not just yet

Isn't it but a dream?
The mere chasing of the wind
Who could tell for sure?

The clock on your wall
It is full of sand
Put your hand in mine
And let us be eternal

You make your own choice now
And throw us between bliss and agony
But I can forgive you

You are so close to death
Yet your eyes so clear
See me

I am ready
And looking for immortality

[Music plays: "Zu Asche, zu Staub" from *Psycho Nikoros*]

I am Althar, the Crystal Dragon.

Unsterblichkeit – *immortality* – *this* is your true nature.

You have *never* been born; you will *never* die. All that happens here, in your human incarnation, is nothing but a dream. Are you chasing the wind? Most surely. Will you ever catch it? *No way.* As long as you run, chasing the wind, you might have interesting experiences, but there's *no way* to overcome death, to go back to your birthright and attain immortality by running or chasing. You cannot *do* it*; you are it already.*

So, I welcome you all back today. As Joachim said, we have a very full plate today. We will start with time. Time in itself is a topic about which we could speak for months and months, until you really, really let go of it. But anyway, we have, say, 45 minutes up to an hour, and we do it just in this short period of no-time.

We put everything in, all the information that might be needed for you – if information is needed at all – but as we said yesterday, so often it starts with a mental concept, because you *are* within the illusion. Then this mental concept grows on you, you accept it, you do not fight it anymore, you do not get impressed by it anymore, and suddenly it becomes a *reality* for you. Sometimes slowly, sometimes in a flickering way. But sooner or later, you will see without a doubt, that *time does not exist.*

Nevertheless, time is one of the greatest inventions that entities in separation ever made. Time allows you to understand what is going on. Time allows you to get a deep understanding by means of repetition and patterns.

You heard me talk in the books about what I call the "now-spheres" or the "scene spheres". A sphere, as you know, is kind of a ball, but sphere is a nicer term. With a now-sphere I denote the sum total of all of your perceptions, interpretations, and feelings you have in any given moment. Just like now. You have the perception and the awareness of the space you're sitting within, of the temperature, of the noises going on, like the fridge working in the background. You hear Joachim's words, you have certain light sensations, you have emotions attached to it, and all the rest of that. Imagine all of this as a 3D photograph and then visualize it with a sphere.

I said that with pure consciousness pondering the thought of separation all of those now-spheres sprang into existence, simultaneously. This is, of course, something that is kind of mind boggling, hard to accept and hard to understand, so I want to explain this a little bit with an analogy. Now, analogies only go so far, otherwise they were the truth, but the one I will choose might make things pretty clear.

So, you all know the game of chess. The game of chess. Take a board with 64 square fields, a number of pieces, and a set of rules. And once you have defined the playground, and the pieces, and the rules – you have *all* potential chess games that could be played. They all exist *immediately!* Can you imagine that?

Because you have only discrete moves with each chess piece according to the rules, you could enumerate all matches immediately. They exist. Now, where are they? Do they exist in some realm? Are they stacked somewhere in a big chess mind somewhere in the universe or in the Akashic chronicles? They are not. They just exist *implicitly*. We have the rules and thereby, *implicitly*, all the potential matches arise.

Now, dive into such a game. Imagine, you are, say, a pawn on the chess board. You are standing there. You are surrounded by other pawns, and behind you there is a queen and the knight and whoever else is around you. You have a certain color, and you move according to your rules. As a pawn, you move usually one field straight forward or sometimes you can kick somebody out if you move diagonally to the left or to the right. This is your world. You see it from there, you experience the battle of the chess game. You might be a very important figure, or you might be sacrificed for some minor tactic, but this is your world. *This*, is your world.

Now think of all the potential chess games that are there. Some are extremely boring, because, say, white is so dominant and black makes all the mistakes it could do, and the game is over very quickly, or it's extremely tense and tight. *So* many potential chess games are there. I'm sure, every one of you has played chess at least once.

Now, if you if you want to enumerate the potential chess games up to 40 moves, you will end up with 10^{115} potential games, this is 1 followed by 115 zeros. They all exist just by defining the rules. They are all there, and you played one or two or maybe even more of those potentials. You enacted them, you dived into them, maybe with somebody else, maybe against a computer. But you have enacted some of those spheres.

Now, if you are getting caught in these games, if you incarnate, say, into a chess figure then you play a game and when it's over you just play the next game according to the rules you have. But which of these tremendously vast amounts of potential games will you enact? Which one do you choose? Where do you go from there? And will you find any differences in the games? Because, in the end, playing chess is always the same. You have the same set of figures, the same feasible moves. Yes, there is a certain suspense and tension, but in the end, isn't it *always* the same? There is *no way* for you *to go beyond playing chess by playing chess.* You have no chance to do that.

Now, let's go further. Imagine we want to represent these matches somehow explicitly, and we have high technology and we say we can represent a complete chess match up to 40 moves in a single atom. We just inscribe it there somehow, energetically. This would mean we would need 10^{115} atoms. Sounds easy. But now your physicists come around and tell you, "I'm... I'm sorry but your physical universe has only 10^{78} atoms." You have not enough atoms in your universe to even enumerate the games of chess up to 40 moves, and there could be many more moves in the game.

So, what do we do? We say, "Pfff, so what, no problem, we just create 10^{37} more universes of the size of this universe so that we can have an explicit representation of all of the chess games." Yesterday we went out and saw many universes. Now imagine you have 10^{37} of them, which is quite a number. And then you know what to do with all those universes – you can represent your chess games, cool, huh?

Now, obviously, there is *no need* to have a presentation of it, there's just no need. *Just by the defining the rules they exist.* And if you're not into chess, *they are so boring.* It's always the same. You can observe it from the outside, and you see those figures moving on this board, forever the same moves, forever the same figures. Yes, each game looks a bit different, but in the end, black is beating white or white is beating black, or you have a truce, and then you continue all over. That is the game of chess.

Now, have a look at separation. You might say separation is also like a game, just like chess. And the good thing about separation is, it has just one rule, *one rule*. The rule is called "separation", and exactly as with chess, everything springs into existence, *immediately*. Maybe it's not as obvious as with chess, but it's the very same principle. One rule: separation.

And separation has certain attributes to it. Separation, of course, knows only separation, and wants ever more separation. So, in a sense, separation cuts itself down into ever smaller pieces. Just like this [claps] – *boom* – in all potential variants, because it can, because it can.

So, just like with the chess games, we instantly have an enormously vast amount of potential now-spheres that could be experienced as separation.

None of them is created from within separation, just as no chess game is created from within chess. It is all implicitly defined by the rules that come from the outside. Now, there's, call it, a *dreaming* portion of pure consciousness, it dreams of separation. This brings forth all the scene spheres of separation.

Then, in a sense, the play begins, you dive into it. You don't even need a physical body because the now-spheres of separation, they contain *everything*, even the times when you weren't in physical form. Everything is already there, but what are you going to experience? Where do you start? How do you move through this *vast* ocean?

66

We have the Atlantic Ocean right at our feet. It's *vast!* Now, imagine each drop of this ocean was in itself an ocean. We have an ocean of oceans, and each drop of these oceans represents a now-sphere that could be experienced. You start somewhere, you dive into a sphere and experience it from within, and it feels real, because for you, when you are in such a sphere, it *is* real! You have perceptions, you have awarenesses, it is kind of cool. But what drives you from one sphere to the next?

Well, over time while you move in these spheres, first randomly, you acquire certain patterns, desires, wishes; you repeat things, create habits, and it is the habits that drives you forward. This is going on until today, until this very moment. You are here, experiencing a now-sphere that has already existed! You've entered here from another sphere and now that you're sitting here, in this tiny fraction of a moment, you have an inward sensation of what's going on, and then you go into the next sphere. The next sphere, not surprisingly, seems to be *very much* like the previous sphere. Why? Because you haven't changed so much. In these small increments, you don't change too much, but you *could*.

Whenever you drop a pattern, *you change the course through the ocean of spheres.* If you drop a pattern, well, it doesn't drive you any longer in the direction it represents, you immediately shift the course. Meaning, the more you let go of whatever, the freer you become. You become ever freer to choose the next sphere to experience to your liking. This is an interesting observation.

When you go into such a new sphere, it cannot be said that you have *created* it. But you have *chosen* it. Seen from within, it appears to you that, ah, here is a new reality and I changed internally, so my outer reflection has changed. Seen from within, this is true. Because seen from within, you might say, well, I've created this, because it is *new* to me. That's true in a sense, but not so true if you are interested in the truth, in the whole picture.

Now, people are running like crazy through those spheres. First, in search of experiences, which is natural, because it is exciting and interesting to just see what's this all about. How can I define myself by means of mirroring myself? By means of patterns and expressions and experiences? That's wonderful.

But then, after a while, let's say, a few eons, you might come to the conclusion that in the end you are merely repeating the same thing. *You're always doing the same.* Yes, there's more variance than in the game of chess, but in the end – there is not so much difference. It *remains* separation. Separation has only one taste. Separation has a taste of repetition, *the taste of repetition*. And it has exactly one driving force. It says "enough is not enough". No matter *what* you do, no matter *how much* you take in, you will never be totally satisfied, at least not in the lasting way. For a small amount of time... yes, you might be saturated, all is well, all is fine. But then something calls you back, and you have to continue the feeding on whatever: food, emotions, sex, you name it. You name it, and you *know* so very well.

Now, here comes the problem. Even though it is so exciting to experience this for a while, just as it is so exciting to experience chess for a while, if you are into it, the question comes up when you see it's just a repetition; I always move the same stupid figures on the same stupid board; I repeat the same stupid experiences, call it love or call it fame, or call it power, or call it whatever… depletion. But after a while, it's not getting just boring, it's *worse*. Because, even if you *want* to get out, if you *want* to stop it – *you don't know how*.

How to get out of here? *How* can I go out of playing chess while playing chess? There's no rule here that allows me to go out of the game. Separation knows only separation. When you have the feeling at some point "*enough is enough*", well, this might be the starting point for the spiritual search. But still, it takes usually a long, long time until these "enough is not enough" has trickled down through all of your various layers. But the question becomes more and more pressing: *How could I ever get out?*

You cannot get out of those spheres by *moving*. One might come up with the idea that there might be this one interesting sphere that finally allows me to go beyond, it might be the exit, so I have to *search* for it. I start traversing all the oceans, all those tiny drops, those now-spheres, searching for that very sphere that allows me to get out. Sometimes you might even have the feeling that you're getting closer. But then, even if you think you are there, a short while later you find yourself yet in another sphere and ask yourself *"What the heck is going on?"*

There is no single now-sphere in separation that is better or worse for leaving than any other. You could leave each and everywhere.

Wherever you are, you could *immediately* exit the dream of separation. As long as you move, as long as you have momentum, you will be propelled through this ocean of now-spheres, searching, running, running after, running away. You really have to realize one thing: It does not matter if you are *going for* something or *denying* something. It doesn't matter – both will propel you forward or backward or sideways.

There's a movement, a momentum within you, there's a desire in you. So, you cannot even *die* yourself out of separation. If you have the *wish* to be out of here, then this very wish, this desire, will move you forward, because you think you can *do* something to make it happen. There's nothing that you can *do*. There's only one thing: *You can let go!* You can *change to the perspective of the Eye of Suchness.*

This is why I've created, or Joachim has created, in a nightlong adventure, this wonderful installation which is placed on the floor showing you a few spheres. A small collection of this vast, vast ocean of spheres.

The symbol here is this: As we are sitting here, you can see those spheres *from the outside*. Yes, of course, they have no explicit representation, but for the sake of our discussion, they are presented explicitly as some small balls or pearls lying on the floor. Imagine you are within one of them and you can choose the next. If you let go of a pattern or of a habit, you can change the direction towards anywhere.

My point is: You can *see* it from the outside and you can *dive in* and experience it from *within*. Seen from within, it is *super real*. Seen from the outside, it is vast, you might marvel at the vast amount of potentials that arise just from the single thought of separation. But you see it also as *what it is*. It is a limited set of storylines that you can travel through. Just like the amount of chess games is vast, but they are limited, and they are always the same. It's just the same with separation.

Now, all entities who entered the dream of separation began within some now-sphere. They started exploring, they started experiencing, and some of them, at some point, *recognized the repetitions*. It took eons and eons, even beyond time, if that makes sense, to come to that conclusion. But now *feel* that. *Feel that. You* have been at that point. You are one of those who have realized this.

How to get out of separation? Because it is always the same. In separation, we have no *real* creation. Here is just *quantity*, here is not a single new *quality*. Yes, a given entity might experience a new quality like hearing beautiful music for the first time, but music as such is not a new quality. Here, it's just quantity – it is more of the same. In other words, we have no *true* creation in separation.

The creation that the entities and the humans have in separation is just entering an already existing sphere for the first time. It was not created by them. It might be visited by a single person or it might be a shared experience with many. Then you get a new trend, a new fashion – it *seems* to be a creation, but in the end it's nothing new.

Look at your mobile phones. Wow, seems like a great creation. But in the end, what do you do with it? Talk bullshit, plainly spoken, most of the time. Exchange stupid pictures. So, why do you need this kind of invention? *Why* do you need this kind of invention if you continue to do the very same things you always did? The fact is, you get more distracted, it's getting ever more complicated. The attention span of the average human is decreasing by the minute. The newborns, the digital natives, they will a have a hard time coming to rest, because they are always in this "What's next, what's next, what's next"-trance. They are so much in the mental. Even if it seems to be a new creation, what do you do with it? *The same old things*, just faster and in a higher resolution.

So, this is the very nature of time. Once you feel you are within a sphere and you go to the next sphere, this is what creates the illusion of time. So time, in a sense, does not exist at all. It is the entity that traverses from sphere to sphere remembering a bit of the "past" and thereby creating its own history. *It creates its own thread of time*, which represents the way that the entity took through this vast, vast, vast ocean of potential now-spheres.

So, let's get a bit more personal, and let's investigate your personal thread of time. To do so I will play a bit of music.

[Music plays]

You are here in this very moment, and whatever you did in this life, whatever you did in *any* life led you to *this* very point. It was like a long march. A long journey. But you ended up in the now, as you always do, and your current now is here, right now. And here you have the chance to *view* the trajectory, your thread of time that you have chosen. To see it from the outside, from the perspective of your true self, just step back. And as you can see this beautiful installation on the floor from the outside, you might see the now-spheres of your current lifetime from the outside. They are connected, they lead "backward in time". Visualize this.

No need to have an infinite number of small spheres that capture each and every minimal fraction of an experience. Just use the most important scenes of your lifetime.

Most certainly, there is your birth. So, see the sphere that marks your birth somewhere in this ocean of now-spheres. Then you grew up. Your first friends. You went to school. First love affairs. See these as small – and they are small, believe me – as small spheres that make up your experiences of this lifetime. Some of you were married or had kids. Maybe you are still married or not.

You might even remember the scene when you heard the call like "Enough is enough, it's time to get out!" It might have changed the course of your life and brought you new experiences. You might have met teachers in person, or in books, or in the etheric realms. All of this changed your course of life. Until you suddenly find yourself in this weird spot, with some weird music playing in the background.

Just feel your personal thread of time. See it from the outside. Isn't it interesting how things have changed? You can glide along your thread of time. Glide backward from the now moment to your birth into this lifetime.

Changing the perspective so often also changes the experiences. You see things that you might have missed when they happened within the spheres. You get a greater understanding.

While you are gliding back, you might see that sphere where you know for sure *this* is where you've heard the call like "Enough is enough, time to get out!" If you so choose, then just radiate this very wish to that you inside that sphere. Tell the young girl or woman, man or boy "All is good. *All* is good. It will work out. Just continue. I know for sure."

Move further back towards your birth.

Oh, the birthing. Becoming connected to the physical. In a sense, with the instant of the inception, there it starts. You are woven into it. You are woven into the DNA, as we will see in the next section, and the DNA replicates, and with the replication your consciousness goes with it. You are woven into it.

Now, from the moment of your birth, *slowly* come back to the now moment, glide along your spheres, along your thread of time, as the wise being that you have become, with the eyes of compassion for yourself. So many important experiences. So many spheres that are apparently not important at all. But who knows, who knows what is hidden there. It may show up only later, or even only from the perspective that you have right now.

Now you arrive at this now moment, and you might ask, "How will I move forward from here?" But before we go forward, let's once again go backward.

We are doing a "belief system stretching". We are stretching the belief in time. On an experiential level, time only moves forward, but here we can go in any direction. We can go backward, forward, even sideways into alternate experiences. But right now, just follow your thread of time once again from the now moment to your birth.

When you're there, just slowly return to the now moment along your thread of time. So many now-spheres. They might have even different colors, shining, they were attractive – why else would you've gone there?

Now, once more, let's go back from the now moment to the sphere of your birthing. Let's stay a moment at that sphere.

You see, you came in with so many expectations, hopes, and wishes. Depending on where in the non-physical you were before incarnating again, you might have had a lot of clarity. But then, when you were birthed into the physical, into the biology – so much was lost... not lost, but *veiled*. You had no access to it. In a sense, you had to relearn. The good thing about consciousness and patterns is that they get easier to use the more often they have been applied. So, the relearning might get ever faster. The remembrance might get deeper, if you are in good circumstances.

Let's go further backward from your birth into the lifetime you've had before. It is just another sphere. Oh, there might be a time in-between where you haven't been in physical form. You might see those spheres where you journeyed in-between your physical lifetimes. Or you might end up on the death bed of your previous lifetime, when you died in that lifetime.

Typically, you had unfulfilled wishes, unfinished business, you had certain fears. All these are driving forces. So, if you are in the physical or not, you are taking your driving forces with you. Some of them fall away, of course, but those that are deep – they go with you. So, it doesn't really matter if you inhabit a physical body or if you are in the non-physical – it is always the same driving forces that move you forward.

There you are, lying on your deathbed, one of so many deaths. Move forward or better…[laughs] backward in time through the life of your previous lifetime. Whatever comes, allow it. If nothing comes, it doesn't matter. Just allow yourself to travel back in time while being beyond time.

You might go back to the birthing of that lifetime. There is no reason to stay there. Just move on. Further. Further and further. How many lives as a human did you have?

Somewhere along this thread of time is your very first incarnation into the human. But there is even a "before that", it didn't start there. Go back. Go further.

You were somewhere in the nonphysical, close to Earth, and prepared yourself for incarnating. Go further. Go further. *Something happened!* We will talk about that in the next session. But let's go further anyway, even if you might feel there is something like a blackness, a shut door, a fear, even guilt. *Move behind that!* Move behind that hidden door, it *cannot keep you out!*

Here you are in the non-physical. Far away. In a very different density as we have here on Earth. Go beyond, and beyond, and beyond.

Go on until you come to the very first experience of "I exist! I don't know who I am, or what I am, or where I am. But *I exist!*" This is where you started. It is one of those spheres in this grand, grand oceans of now-spheres of separation. Can you see that thread of time?

See the Atlantic Ocean, representing an ocean of now-spheres. Imagine there is a thread connecting some drops, representing your thread of time. It might be a long thread, a winded thread. Most certainly you have not visited all possible drops. But you know for sure, the drops, the now-spheres that you have not visited yet are not *so* different from those you have visited.

Time is a flexible thing, isn't it?

Now, let's do an experiment. Arrange this

thread of time that you see in front of you into a spiral. You are in the center and all the spheres that make up your thread of time smoothly arrange themselves into a spiral. A spiral that is going outward, outward into infinity. You are, in a sense, like the central sun of your lives, of your experiences.

Now, it's interesting that humans so often hope for the future. They *hope* that the future may bring the revelation, salvation, enlightenment. But what about the past? *What about the past?* If it is the attachments that are manifesting the patterns, the hidden fears, guilt, shame, and wishes that propel you through your experiences... for sure, they have been acted out and have been acquired in the past. So why not change the past? Why not *heal* the past? Would you do the same things again that you did having the knowingness that you have now?

There's absolutely no judgment in this. It's just the way to accumulate wisdom, for how could you know what would be the right thing in the long run. Just assume you always did the best you could. And you did, otherwise you would not be here, right?

Now, let's visualize you being in the center and all the spheres of all of your lifetimes arrange in a spiral around you, and you just radiate out: "It's okay. It is just okay. This is a dream in separation. This was all just experience. Whatever happened, whatever appeared to have happened did not *really* happen. We were all just going into certain spheres that already existed. We brought them to life by experiencing them from within."

We now come to a conclusion, a resume.

Here we are in the Second Round of Creation. We feel the standstill in every pore of our existence. There is just repetition, no true creation. And the wisdom is: Oh, we cannot get out here by *moving,* or even by *choosing*, or by *improving*, or by rituals, or by prayers, or by higher deities. They do not exist. You've been everywhere or close to everywhere, but you have never met any such being, right? Did you? But you have heard of true wisdom. The true wisdom that allows you to go beyond, that allows you to shift the perspective from within the now-spheres to the outside. *To see things as they are.*

Radiate *that* out, and see how the spiral rearranges, how you changed the past. For the past is nothing fixed. What you've experienced is not written in stone. As the wisdom goes out, you *reinterpret* your own past, even the occurrences in this lifetime. What you thought was foolish back then, you now understand as great wisdom, because it brought you somewhere, to an insight, brought you to true wisdom.

As you radiate this insight out, true wisdom permeates throughout all of the spheres of all of your lifetimes, and alien lifeforms, and whatever form you have taken on. If they so choose, they can apply the true wisdom onto their own experiences, they can let go of so many things.

Is there a need to heal the past? Surely not. Surely not. Any entity, every entity could leave the world of separation *immediately* by just letting go of the belief in separation. It is *absolutely* possible. However, empirically it happens very seldomly, because separation feels so real, it is so seducing, and there are very strong attachments. So, we need to have mechanisms, helping tools, helpful means like this to allow yourself to forgive you for what you have never done. Isn't that strange? But you know what, *it truly works.*

See once again the totality of the oceans of now-spheres. They do not have an explicit representation. They are created instantly by a single rule, but you can visualize them as if they would exist.

Such is the nature of time – it does not exist.

Having this broad perspective, you even see that what the humans call energy does not exist. Within a single sphere, where is the energy? It is a static thing, and then you move on to the next sphere, and to the next, and you have small changes.

Seen from within, you might say, okay, here is a car in this position, there's a car in that position, so there's a certain energy that moves the car from here to there. But energy *as such* does not exist. So, energy is just an abstraction, a way to describe changes within your now-spheres. There's no *force* to energy, as you can see from the outside, seen as it truly is. So why would you want to be able to *command* energies? They do not exist. Just choose your now-spheres, go where you like, let go of the patterns, *let go of your belief in energy and see what happens.* This might free you from so many limitations.

A word of caution. It might well be that people come across this message, be it in the audio or in the books. And they use this information to search for the final ultimate experience, that single now-sphere somewhere in the ocean that fulfills them, huh, in unbelievable ways. *It doesn't work that way.* Oh, go there, yes, if you really want to do it, *do not suppress it.* If you have *unfulfilled wishes* within separation, by all means, *follow them, do not hold back.* Really, *do not hold back!*

Only if you have realized within yourself "enough is enough", only then will the information that is coming through right now unfold on you. Until then, it will be a potential that you can tap into anytime as a remembrance. But as long as you suppress anything, as long as you feel a certain shame, because you *want* something, whatever it is – this momentum will keep you from realizing the full broadness of what I've just laid out.

But even then, have the compassion for yourself, because there are many, many, many small driving forces within you that you are not yet aware of. They also keep you back, they play out on a micro level of your consciousness.

So, even if you truly feel that on the higher level of your consciousness that it's okay, that you are at peace with separation, you do not need anything, which doesn't mean that you cannot enjoy things. But you don't *need* to chase them or *reject* them, you are *free* to experience. But still, sometimes, you find yourself back in the limited human mode. There are additional deep reasons on the micro level that are causing this, and we will go into them in the next section.

For now, once again, embrace all of these spheres of separation. There's nothing good or bad here. *Nothing*. It is just *as it is*. There was not a single wrong choice you've ever made. You just went into now-spheres that already existed.

Slowly come back to the now moment. You might bow to all of you, to all you have experienced, to all of your lifetimes. They greet you, they feel relieved, they've gained a deeper understanding.

Come back to this now moment in Cascais, in the year of 2019.

What about the future, you might ask? What about the future? Well, we could do what we just did, like… imagine your future. Moving forward, dying, moving forward, dying. But I leave that up to you. Ask yourself in a silent moment: What do you want your future to be? How do you want to experience it? Imagine you were free of *any momentum*, free of any limitation. What sphere in separation would you *like* to experience? Or is it that the current given moment you are in, is perfect as it is? There's no right or wrong answer. You're free. You're free to bring this in.

You're free to let go of your past. You can *cut* the thread of your time, for instance, right now! You see! Say goodbye to your previous incarnations. *Cut the link.* Release *them*. And with them you might release so many patterns that carried over from them.

In the end, you are not there anyway. You are on the outside, just projecting some part of your consciousness into those spheres. You have no obligation. None whatsoever. *None whatsoever.* You are a free, sovereign being. *Maybe it's time to come to realize this.*

I am Althar, the Crystal Dragon. It was a great pleasure for me to be with you beyond time. I will see you in a few minutes, whatever that means.

5. Consciousness and Matter – The Lord of Death – Releasing Uru

I am Aouwa.

I am the beginning, the end, and the beyond of all that is. Now comes a point in your linear time that I've been waiting a long, long time for. I invite you to come with me on a journey to a point where, in a sense, things began anew.

We will go back to a time before the decision was made to incarnate in the physical.

Here, in our gathering in Portugal, we have spoken about the standstill a couple of times, and I've written about it. The standstill meaning the realization that there is no true creation in separation. Only repetitions.

Realizing this is indeed terrifying. And when enough true selves, enough families realized this, they came together to find a way out, and as you know, one idea was to go by way of physical matter.

I have spoken of the family of Uriel and a subbranch of it called Uru. Uru is also known as a group of the "master scientists". Just as all of Uriel, they've chosen to stay as close to pure consciousness as possible. Most others ventured out and explored all kinds of experiences in separation, all the variations. But Uru, the entities of Uru, they were intrigued by the question "*How* does this all work? This, where we find ourselves in."

Back then we – because I was among them – we had no clue of separation. We didn't have the notion of separation. We weren't yet aware of this concept. We explored *how* this all comes into existence. We were longing for what we have lost, for what we have felt we were lacking – the true peace within. We *wanted* to go back.

So, while the others went out to explore and to play all kinds of... call it games, but it's not meant in a derogatory way, we approached it from a very observative standpoint. And very soon, sooner than most others, we came across this thing, called the standstill. We observed the others, we heard them talk, we heard them exchange, and because we were not so much with them but more outside of them, it was easier for us to become aware of the repetitions, to see the patterns.

So, "*How* to get out?" – that was our quest. And we've experimented. We experimented a lot. Quite soon we discovered the possibility of what is now called "to go within." Not going so much into the *outside*, into the outside mirroring of yourself, into the outside expression but, in a sense, to ponder and to observe what is going on *within*.

We went deeper and deeper, trying to understand where we were, how we could get out, how this thing "creation" worked at all. How it could be that we lacked something?

While going within, we also noticed in an experiential way, that when applying separation on separation we could create something that is denser. Call it a denser consciousness, if that makes any sense. So, we went into ever deeper densities, exploring them, observing what's going on there.

At some point, we had the truly bright idea that... what if we can go so deep that we forget where we came from? Then, if we can find a way back, this then might be the trigger for us on the higher level of consciousness to also go back to where we came from.

So, while the others were playing the energy games, we went deep and deeper, and denser and denser using a technique you would call "compression". We compressed our consciousness to ever deeper levels. But, we found out that even though we did the compression and even though an entity that has undergone the compression found itself in a different state, in a different knowingness, it was not *difficult enough* for the entity to come back, to find its way back.

So, the entities of Uru that went deep into density had kind of interesting experiences, but it was quite easy or not difficult enough for them to come back, so that when they came back, they had the experience of letting go, which is a fundamental important experience, but it did not resolve *all doubt* they had about the experience. In a sense, you might say, the density was not deep enough, things happened *too fast* to really explore cause and effect. So, there was a remainder of doubt.

This is what I've called "the principle of ascension". We *knew* about the principle, but it didn't go all the way, it didn't go all the way.

Back then, we tried to talk to others about the standstill, but they weren't ready to hear. Well, it is like today, it's always the same – some are ready, most are not. But back then, after a long, long time, suddenly there was a critical mass of entities that agreed that the standstill was all around. And then we pondered various ideas of what can be done.

So, the idea came up to try to bring consciousness into physical matter, for physical matter was the highest density that we knew of. But then, as bright as that idea was, the question came up immediately, "How could consciousness and physical matter be reconciled? How could they merge or meld?" They are like fire and water, they just do not fit together. The underlying hope was, when being in the belief of being such a slow-motion entity within a physical body and having the realization of letting go, that would also trigger an insight on the level of the true self.

So, in this great gathering that we were at, the entities and the other families where at a loss. "What could we do to bring consciousness into matter?" So Uru stepped forward. They hesitated for quite a while before doing so, because they knew what they would propose would bring them into a position that would be quite difficult. But, as they also knew, the standstill was not a fiction but real, they had chosen to be in service. So, they stepped forward and talked about the research they had conducted over such a long period of time. They spoke about the principle of ascension. They spoke about why they thought it did not work, and then they proposed to do the very same with the consciousness that wanted to incarnate into physical matter. That means, they laid out the process of "compression". First, the compression.

Now, yesterday you travelled into an atom. You explored the energies that are working on that level. We had the example of an atomic explosion once you tear apart the nucleus of an atom. Now, talking about compression, sounds like fun, but I tell you... imagine an atomic explosion. You've all seen the mushroom clouds. Such a great phenomenon coming from such a small, small amount of atoms. Now imagine, you are such a mushroom cloud, and you want to go back into the physical matter, like reversing the process. This is a compression. This means, we apply the force of an atomic explosion to consciousness, so we have, say, a *consciousness implosion*. But the consciousness implosion has the same magnitude as an atomic explosion – it is grand. It sounds like adventure, but it is certainly not fun.

Uru had gone quite deep, and with all the research they had done, they noticed that this might not even suffice. They knew that when going in deeper densities, you will *veil* your consciousness. You will not be able to sense or remember your true self. The density is veiling a lot of aspects of yourself. But this in itself would not suffice for you to really bond with the physical. By applying the consciousness implosion, the compression, you become very much like the physical, very dense, but still you are not physical.

And so they said, an additional *hypnosis* was required. A hypnosis on a part of your consciousness that is already compressed so that is *craves*, that it *longs* to bond with the atoms, so that it eventually *clings* to the nucleus with the same force as the neutrons and protons cling together. This consciousness should become similar to iron ore. Like stone with some iron in it. The iron in itself *feels* like the stone surrounding it. It is still different, but it thinks it's the same, it's cold, it's heavy, it's surrounded by it, the iron *believes it is of stone*. So, that was the intention with hypnotizing that portion of consciousness; to go so deep into matter, into the physical subatomic particles and to bond with the same strength that the particles do, to become like matter, to be under this spell, under the belief of being matter.

So, that was the idea, the suggestion Uru brought forth. And as you might imagine, huh, in an abstract way it sounds interesting. But who wants to step forward and apply an atomic explosion onto itself? But Uru was amongst the first to step forth, they volunteered. And as they did, others came forth also. This was the first wave, the "first wavers", and it is likely that some of you might have been amongst them.

Uru stated explicitly they had *no clue* if this

would work and that there was a big potential that whoever went there might be crippled for eternity. For a part of the consciousness of the true self would be, in a sense, split apart, ripped apart, hypnotized into believing itself to be matter. And the hypnosis, that was one condition, needed to be irreversible from the outside. There was no way that any entity other than the incarnated entity could release the hypnosis. Otherwise, all kinds of problems would have arisen. The families were in energy games and wars for eons, so imagine what would happen if somebody had the key to release the entities. Not good for the overall approach that we had.

So, we had the first wavers. They were ready to come in. Uru knew that the role they were playing was harsh. They were taking on the role of the "bad boy". You see, there was another role, the role of Gaia. Because at that point, there were no biological organisms, there was no Earth. There was just a rock somewhere in outer space that needed to be impregnated with life force energies. The biological forms needed to be brought forth, they had to be dreamt into existence. This was kind of the positive way, Gaia was, so to speak, "the good guy". And someone had to play "the bad guy", Uru, for Gaia alone, just bringing forth organisms, would not have sufficed to merge them with the high consciousness of the true selves.

Now imagine, even if you were not amongst the first wavers, a part of you, some previous incarnation at some point in time did his or her or its first trip to Earth. So, metaphorically speaking, you entered a compression chamber and Uru was the last you have seen. Uru was the one who had locked the door. Uru was the one who started the compression. And the compression was not nice, it was *certainly* not nice. It went stronger, and stronger, and stronger. Not just one atomic explosion, but one after the other. Always, always, always compressing the consciousness more and more. While you were in that compression chamber, you quickly forgot *why* you were there and a doubt came up within you, "*I must have done something wrong. Why the hell would anybody treat me like this?*" All the noble causes that you might have had were *squeezed* out of you. You did not know them anymore. You just knew the torture, the compression and you felt "*I must have done something wrong*", and therefore, in a sense, "*I must deserve this treatment*". It was the initial shame and guilt that came with the compression.

When the compression was ready, the hypnosis was applied onto a part of your consciousness, onto a part of your already compressed consciousness. You might say that this part then truly, truly longed and craved to bond with the physical. In a sense, it was as split-off from the rest of your human consciousness, as the human consciousness was split-off from its true self.

But the compression did not directly, say, pump you into a physical body. You started out as an etheric being, getting used to the physical world, and you bonded with the animals and plants. But when you, at some point in time, were trapped into a physical birth through an entity, *then* the hypnosis *really* snapped. It snapped into the DNA of that entity, on the level of the atoms, right where we were yesterday. *It clicked,* and from that moment on you were *locked into the biology* and the cycle of physical birth and death.

You might say, this was a triumph, for embodiment was *very* difficult. On the other side, there was a big "Hurray!" and a big party when this portion of the plan worked out.

But, it also meant that now you were truly locked into the physical, and Uru was the one who has locked the door. By that time, you most certainly had forgotten Uru and its name, but there's an innate fear that you carry with you since you have undergone that compression treatment.

The fear is that you might meet Uru again. You might meet Uru again, if you ever try to release that bond with the physical. Can you feel that? Can you imagine that?

You've undergone what you felt was a big torture, suddenly you were out of the torture chamber and you kind of forgot about it. But the torturer is somehow around. You can't see him. He is not visible to you, but he's a spook. He is in your dreams, he haunts you at night, he lurks in the dark corners of your cellar. He is the Lord of Death. That is what Uru represents to those who are, in a sense, damned into eternity to be within the physical. An eternal prison. *How to get out of it?* The door is hidden, locked and sealed, and if you ever find it, then Uru awaits you in the dark – and Uru most certainly has another nice treatment for you, if you plan to get out, or so goes the thinking.

The fear is deep, it's deep. It's deep on the very biological level, on the physical level. You have a lot of fears and guilt and shame and what not on the higher levels of your consciousness, but deep down there is this tremendous, tremendous fear. *Letting go of the physical is equivalent to meeting Uru again*, to be back in his hands. No way to escape. Ready for another nice treatment. Feel for a moment what that means. What would you do if you had such a burden, such a memory?

As harsh as it sounds, this is exactly how it was intended to be, for the plan was to truly mimic what the true selves felt when they went into separation. The true selves, in a sense, they were ripped apart into fragments. Into so many fragments, into the fragments of separation itself. Can you feel that? Doesn't feel very good either. We weren't so much aware of it, but now we know. But when it happened, it was awful. Humans would call it painful. The soul was ripped apart, in a sense, and then forgotten. Then suddenly, you started out in some of those tiny spheres and began your journey through separation. Through Uru, your last remembrance of your true self, of who you were and who you are, was *squeezed* out of you, *sucked* out of you.

So, you found yourself in the very same condition as your true self back then, but in an *ultra* slow-motion environment, ready to explore cause and effect. Ready to explore what you call energy, ready to explore what it means to *do* something and to observe the resulting effect. And because it is such slow motion, and because of the wonders of patterns and repetitions, you repeated the experiences so often until you finally understood.

Now you might see why attempting to leave the physical triggers the fear of meeting Uru. But before the fear there's even a layer of guilt and shame, and you know what humans do or any entity does with guilt and shame. Of course, they suppress it and deny it. They arrange their life and their experiences so as to never be exposed to them. It's like a magnet within that pushes you into directions where you do not have to feel it, where you do not have to see it. You *just don't go* where you are exposed to this shame and guilt.

For instance, take your physical body. Almost no human is really happy or unashamed with his physical body, never. That's why they wear clothes, even if it's hot like crazy. Why is that? It is shame and they don't even notice it. They just find situations where they are not exposed to the shame, and they don't even notice that. Thus, if you want to get out of separation and still carry shame and guilt with you, well, you will not come too far. You have to face it. You truly have to face it.

This is why the dragons are coming in. They help you. *Finding* that. *Showing* that. *Accepting* that. That's why we did the exercises yesterday.

95

The dragon, in a sense, is a *representation* of Uru, a gentler variant of Uru. You can accept the dragon *easier* than Uru, but the dragon is strong in itself, and it shows you all the shame, guilt and all the things you do not want to see within yourself.

How could you meet Uru if you are a shambles, without self-worth or dignity? Frightened of things to come that you cannot even see. It doesn't work. If there's this layer of guilt and shame within you, you will not even *approach* the hidden door. So, the dragon comes in, sent, when the human asks for it and is ready for it. The dragon comes in, *and it points out* the dark spots that you do not want to see, so as to make you ready for the true thing. This is not a question of a one-time encounter, like, "Oh, I've met the dragon and I looked him or her into the eyes and suddenly I'm clear of everything." That's crap. This goes deep, and as we will see, it also goes into the micro level of consciousness, into the micro level of consciousness.

The consciousness that has connected so deeply with the physical matter, built-up from there, and it made its way through the molecules into the cells. Now imagine a single cell. There is your consciousness within, and your consciousness down there believes *it is* this cell. The cell wants to survive, the cell wants to reproduce, and the cell wants to feed. This is what's going on at the level of a cell. Your hypnotized consciousness is down there, and it believes it is a cell, it wants exactly this – survive, in the end. It does not ponder questions of the standstill, it doesn't care if there's evolution on that level, no, no. It is hypnotized into believing "I am just this, I am a tiny cell". And you have plenty of them. 10^{14} cells.

Now, here you go with your *higher* level of consciousness. You've heard of enlightenment, and you want to let go of the physical. It appears to even work for a while, even an hour or so. But when it becomes *real*, you have quite a mass with you, the mass consciousness of your cells, that has a different opinion than you have. This is the rubber band that pulls you back. When the consciousness in the cells sense that you are about to leave, *they fear death.* They want just one thing – they want to survive.

You want to see how that feels? Stop breathing, now!

*

You see, stopping breathing is cool in the beginning, then it becomes quite uncomfortable, and then the physical body takes over. If you go "out there", it's cool in the beginning, after a while it becomes uncomfortable, and then the physical body calls you back. So, what needs to be done is not only a release of shame and guilt on the higher levels of consciousness, but we also have to go deep, deep, deep into the physical and release the fear of death.

You see, this is also the reason why an arbitrary normal human who is about to die, because he's terminally ill and even old, and in physical pain. Even if he wants to die, he doesn't arrive at it. It's so difficult. As long as the body can survive *somehow,* it calls the consciousness back. Because there is that deep, deep belief of "I am a body". And right behind that door is the fear of meeting Uru, of being judged, of being sent to have yet another nice treatment.

Actually, there are a few things that can be done about this. On the level of the physical, you can wake up the consciousness that is bound there. We will dive into that in the afternoon. But on a more psychological level, concerning all that happened through Uru and the role Uru has played, it is important to shift your perspective to what really happened.

You see, no matter if you are aware of it or not, it is a deep trauma within you. Nobody takes a couple of atomic explosions with a smile. It just doesn't happen. So, you have to release the fear that this might happen again. One helpful tool to do so... and I say helpful tool, because there is not only one solution for all. If there's a trauma, then some procedures might work for one person and other procedures for other people. But there's one thing that is in general very helpful, and this is what we did in the previous session: Shifting your perspective to what really happened.

See that you have undergone this treatment voluntarily. You have agreed to it. You said, "Yes, I will do it." And Uru was amongst you. Members of Uru came with you. You are equals.

So, Uru together with Gaia, together with those who came first, they've enabled incarnation as such. Uru is *in no way* the Lord of Death, or the torturer, or the eternal guardian of the hidden door of your prison. Instead, Uru is a bearer of light, as close to consciousness as possible. He has shared his wisdom and expertise with all those who were interested. He dived with you into the adventure.

I, Aouwa, as a member of Uru, I tell you – there is no such treatment awaiting you behind the hidden door. You release the physical and you will be in *absolute* liberation. In absolute liberation. I, Aouwa, plant this deeply within you.

As you approach the final letting go, many, many fears will come up that you have not yet experienced. Some of them are obscure, you cannot really put your finger on them, because so much of what happened to you in the past, when you were murdered or died a horrible death, you equated it with Uru waiting for you. Now, that you have a broader perspective; now, that you are able to see the past as it truly was, *you can heal that.*

It doesn't mean that the fear is gone, but it might remind you that when you sense the fear you can shift the perspective and just breathe it in. You do not argue with it. You do not fight it. You do not pity yourself. You just go into remembrance, and then you recall why you came here. You came here in a quest for going beyond, for resolving the standstill. That is what we call ascension.

The human who is finally able to let go of the belief in separation – a belief that made itself so strong by applying separation to itself over and over again – the human who goes beyond separation liberates not only itself, but, in a sense, all of existence. For, if there is no separation, where does the true self end and the rest begin?

I also tell you: *It has already happened!* The first being that realized ascension helped to overcome the standstill. For then it was known, "Y*es, there's still creation and it was never gone, it was just veiled.*" It is just a residual of consciousness playing in the now spheres of separation. The aftermath, so to speak, of a bad dream.

Seen from beyond time, it didn't take any time at all, it was just a thought that occurred. The thought of separation sprang into existence, and it was overcome immediately, for it was so unnatural.

Yet, still you are here and this all sounds very nice, and you might want to believe it. But in the end, the story that we tell ourselves, or the story that you believe in or want to believe in, is not really so important. For the answer, no matter what your story is, is to go *beyond* your story. To go beyond your story, you have to shift the perspective! You have to apply the Eye of Suchness and thus overcome each and every story. We use illusions to overcome illusions. This is the deepest truth.

We traveled together through the second round of creation. The way we experienced it is captured by the story I've told. There are other stories, other experiences. None is better than the other. But you, sitting here, you might see the truth in it, you might feel the truth in it, and it might help you to let go of whatever comes in terms of fear or resistance. You *accept* everything, as the dragon did yesterday. Call it forgiveness. Forgiveness for things you have never done, because those spheres of separation where already there, they were not created by you. You are just a visitor, you have always been.

I said in the beginning that Uru is present in this meeting, not just through me but there are other entities. Entities that have ascended, they made it. They're ready to assist you, just like the dragon. They cannot do it for you, but they can comfort you, you can see them as they are. They bless you.

Also, as a member of Uru, of course, all of existence, all of the entities are interested in making this transition *smoother*, making it easier. This is why I say and others say, every breath you take as a human with the knowingness that you have now, *you help to create the new blueprints*, the new templates, the new patterns, so that others who come after you can find the easy way more easily.

Now that we know, now that true wisdom is present, now that true wisdom is applied more and more often, *even* in the physical, now that enlightened beings keep staying on Earth, it becomes easier for all of the others. Every human who has a moment of enlightenment and radiates it *changes all of existence, changes the course of all true selves.* You may not notice, but you highlight the potential of openness, of acceptance, of compassion, of shifting the perspective to the Eye of Suchness, of seeing things as they are.

So, in that respect, it is absolutely not a question of time or of speed when you will finally, eventually, get beyond the physical. It is not about you anymore. You made it already. Your physical, your human that is walking the Earth right now creates the templates for the new ones. You pave the way, the easy way, for why, oh why would an entity have to undergo so much, call it suffering, and blindness, and numbness, until it finally comes to the point where it is able to release the belief in separation.

That is the nature of Uru: researching, moving forward, making things simpler. So Uru, in a sense, is your best friend. With that I invite you to internally release Uru from the spell of being the Lord of Death and the torturer.

You see, becoming consciously aware of the role of Uru also has an imprint on the overall blueprints of humanity, of those incarnated. It makes it easier for the others to see things as they truly were.

So, whenever you encounter the darkness within, whenever you enter the void, the absence of perception and fear comes up, equate it with joy. The joy that enlightenment is just a breath away. There's no need for any fear here, no, none whatsoever, quite to the contrary.

So, on behalf of the group of Uru, I thank you for being here, for being part of this, for having heard the call. By the way, it might well be that one or another of you is also from that very same group.

And in the name of myself, of Althar, and of Joachim, I herewith state, "I fulfilled my promise!"

Thank you.

6. Veiling – The Light Body Exercise

[Music plays: "Dream",
from *Imagine Dragons*]

I am Althar, the Crystal Dragon!

"I want to dream", we have just heard. "Everything is a just a dream. We are living in a dream. And everything is actually a mess." So thinks the author of this song from the wonderful group called *Imagine Dragons*.

It appears that all the answers are omnipresent, it seems that everybody knows innately "We are living in a dream." But most often there is just the wrong conclusion – the author here says, he *wants* to dream, he wants to *continue* dreaming. And if he wants to dream, a *nicer* dream, a dream that plays out more on the sunny side of polarity – he will get it. He will *continue* to dream.

There's a wonderful poem, the Shin Jin Mei, from a great Zen master by the name of *Sosan*. In this poem it is said:

If the Eye of Suchness does not sleep, the various dreams cease.

Just so! The *various* dreams cease. The human in particular is dreaming on so many levels simultaneously. He is dreaming on his mental level, having all kinds of thoughts. He is dreaming on his emotional level, he is dreaming on his physical level. You could bring in many more levels where we have kind of independent existences. Everywhere, on all these various levels, dreams are going on. They fight for attention. They fight each other. They try to push away each other.

Once in a while, everything seems to be in alignment. Once in a while, just like on a cloudy day, the clouds make room for the light to shine through and suddenly, you can see the sun. But actually, the sun was always there. It was just *veiled* by the clouds.

Because there are so many layers of clouds at different altitudes, you seldom get to see the sun, although it is never gone.

We have already spoken many words, and if words could help you to let go of separation, things would be very easy. But unfortunately, as you know, even the wisest words spoken usually do not suffice. There are exceptions, but even those exceptions are not *really* exceptions, because if it *appears* that something like "instant enlightenment" happened then it is only because there was a long, long preparation before.

So, the words alone do not suffice. The true wisdom alone needs to become a *lived* experience. And the easiest way, maybe the only way even, is by way of *practicing*.

I spoke at length about the practice of cultivating your awareness, cultivating *being present*. If you cultivate being present in the sense that you just *observe* whatever is going on, you let go. You let it pass. You realize you are *not it;* you are not *in* it.

If you do that, you can step out of the movie that you are just seeing. You are not *bound* any more to reactions, but now you can *act*. You can decide freely *not* to continue whatever has been going on. You can just observe. You can let it go.

By the way, what you can perceive, what you can be aware of *is not you, cannot be you.*

So, just doing this will inevitably lead you to enlightenment. It has been done throughout the ages, everywhere. Oh, you might find all kind of names for it, like "going within", "observe", "being aware of your awareness", "let go of whatever you perceive",... and at some point, you will become enlightened.

If that happens, if you make it through all your fears and let them go, through your guilt and shame and let them go, if you let go of whatever crosses you inner awareness – if that truly happens, if you let go of the belief in separation, then you are faced with the question, "What next?"

Do you want to stay here, inside a human body, in an environment that is raw, harsh and in the deepest sense of the word *unnatural*? Or do you just exit the dream of separation and go back to your true home, to your true *you*?

This is up to you. There is no obligation whatsoever. But the fact is that most people who come to this point are so compelled by, say, the bliss from beyond that they just leave. They see no reason to stay and to be ridiculed if they try to share their wisdom, being crucified, being stoned to death. You name it, what happened in the past and still happens in quite a number of areas in the world. Even in your western societies, it is certainly not easy to live this, to speak about it or even to bear the mass consciousness that is all around you. Thus, many choose to leave and this is the very reason why there are so few enlightened beings around.

Some did stay, for instance, Buddha. He stayed 45 years after his enlightenment. He taught, he spoke on all levels of depths to those who came to him, he always spoke on the level that could be understood by the person he was talking to. But Buddha had a good setup. He was accompanied by a few others who were really amongst the deepest humans who have ever walked on planet Earth. So, they were a group of enlightened beings, sharing the journey together. Also, they were in an environment that was open to spirituality. Even though they were kind of rebels, having different notions than the classical religion of their time, the overall consciousness was to be open to discussion, to be open and to reflect. So, this was a blessing of Buddha's time, even though it was not always easy. But coming to enlightenment back then had a higher probability.

Others who did it were shielded in monasteries, or they lived secluded in sanctuaries or isolated spots just to be on their own or with just a few disciples.

So, being enlightened and staying on Earth is not an easy thing, so many choose just to leave.

Now, the means to stay, if you so choose, is to prepare a vessel of yourself which is called a "light body". The light body is very different from the physical body. First of all, you have to understand that the light body is created on the level of the true self. It is an *intent* held on the level of your true self.

You may see it as a conscious projection of your true self into the world of separation. As such, it is *immediately perfect!* It doesn't have to learn anything! It is just there. However, there is the physical and the residuals of the attachments of the incarnated human that are still hanging on to the physical body. Thus, the question is, "How can the consciousness shift gracefully from the physical into the light body?" Shifting does not mean to give up the physical body, but it means to make the light body the center of your awareness in this reality. This is the light body, and the physical body will become an extension of it.

You see, just like your mind moves your hand... you might say, in a sense, your hand is an extension of your mind as it follows your intents. The very same thing will happen with the totality of your physical body – it can follow the intent of your light body, of *you!* Of the you that you truly are. It is still possible then to interact with other people through your physical body without feeling the tremendous harshness of physical reality that you had to endure if you only had your physical body. This is the whole idea.

As I have said, you do not shift instantly into your light body, specifically for the reason I have laid out in the previous session. Namely, that you are *tightly woven into* your physical body. Hence, the shifting into your light body *has* to take time. You are in a deep, deep sleep on that level. In a sense, you are dreaming to be physical and it is not about shaking you up with a rude awakening. It is a deep dream, not always a pleasant dream. You want to wake yourself up softly to gently switch into your light body.

So, just as cultivating your awareness leads to enlightenment, cultivating the light body allows you to simultaneously come to enlightenment *and* to prepare the light body, so you have an easier choice to stay on Earth in the world of separation. You do it simultaneously.

If your enlightenment comes too early, then you might have a very difficult time and just switch sides, which is okay, but maybe not what you have chosen. Thus, you do both. You prepare your light body. You get used to it. You find trust in it. You slowly release the consciousness that is woven into your physical body and let it slowly shift and awaken to your true reality, which is your light body – a conscious projection into the world of separation.

As with cultivating your awareness, cultivating your light body is *not* a doing. You do not "create" the light body. It is *not* in your human control how the process works out in detail. *Not at all!* The reason is simply that the light body is already there in perfection. It is all around you, and then the physical body mimics what is all around it. This is what the physical body always does. It *mimics* what is all around it. This is also what your hypnotized consciousness on the physical level does – it mimics the physical matter, because it is all around it.

This goes slowly. So, the only thing you actually do is *stop doing*. You allow yourself the time to be present in your awareness and to be present in your light body. Then you take advantage of something that, again, is not a doing, but a realization of a fact that is so very helpful in the process of shifting the consciousness into the light body.

That is the very fact that what the human in the end *really* wants is to *feel* is a certain feeling. Think of it, whatever you do in your daily life, why do you do it? Because when whatever you try to do is realized, you have a certain feeling within – that's why you do it. You want to have that feeling, whatever the feeling is. This is not good, this is not bad, this is just a fact.

Now, imagine you could bring forth a feeling *without any outer stimulation.* Can you imagine that? You have the desire for something and instead of going outward, trying to setup the right circumstances so that the feeling is triggered from the outside, you could just bring forth the feeling from within in whatever intensity you choose. Then what you felt as a desire is satisfied, and because it is unconditioned from the outside – feel into that – *unconditioned* from the outside, *it can be satisfied forever,* or as often as the desire shows up.

This an observation that is tremendously helpful for everything. Imagine how free you would be in your life if you knew every desire, which is just the wish to experience a certain feeling, could be instantly satisfied by yourself. In that moment, *you would be absolutely free!* In a sense, all of your patterns exist to either *provide* you with a certain feeling or to *avoid* a certain feeling through outer circumstances. Now all of this vanishes. They are not required any more. If there is still a craving for something within, you can notice it and bring forth the feeling to satisfy it immediately.

By doing so, you do *not enact* the pattern that created the desire, and thus, you take off the energy and momentum from that pattern. Therefore, the deconditioning takes place, the pattern will vanish.

Now, we bring all of this into the light body exercise, knowing that this exercise is not about perfecting yourself or improving yourself – *it is a coming back to your natural state.* To make that as clear as possible, let's find a term for the feeling you have when you are in your natural state. From your human perspective, you might say that in your natural state all feelings are combined that you as a human would term pleasant. You might feel peace, beauty, love, safety, completion – you name it. Whatever you term as pleasant is within your true nature, it is already there, it is *innate.*

It is like the white light that contains all the colors you see. The term I use for this combination of all pleasant feelings is "bliss". You can use any other term; the term as such is not important, but just to have a name, I use bliss. It is important to know that the bliss I'm speaking of is not exhausting you.

There are certain kinds of beautiful experiences that are exhausting. You cannot stand them for too long. The bliss of your natural state is *natural,* it is non-exhausting.

So, when you are in the state of your true state and you bring forth your light body, *it is filled with bliss.* It surrounds your physical body, it engulfs you and then what happens is: Your physical body takes notice, "Oh, there is bliss!" and with the bliss come all the individual feelings that are contained in it.

Before we go deeper into the details, let's come back to what we have discussed in the previous session with the compression and the veiling. The fact is that as you compress consciousness into a lower vibration, you veil the ability of being aware of certain feelings that are present in the totality of bliss. Suddenly, the veiled feelings are *lacking.* Then you go to the next compression level, and again something seems lacking, you cannot perceive it any more. And so forth, and so forth.

Now, let's feel into the following series of feelings. We start with *bliss*. Yesterday, some of you experienced the Trinity, being full and complete. This might be bliss for you, a wonderful feeling of "fullness". Then feel into *clarity*. Feel clarity. The next is: *love,* or unconditional acceptance, total acceptance. The last is: *safety.*

These four feelings correspond to the four core levels of your existence as a human. The bliss is on the level of your true self. Clarity on the level of the mental. Love or total acceptance on the level of the emotional – or the emotional body and the mental body. And then you have safety on the level of the physical body.

When the compression took place, it started on the highest level and then went down, down, down to the physical level. As soon as the compression arrives at the mental level, you feel a *lack* – something is veiled. What is veiled here is the clarity. The interesting thing is, on the level of bliss, on the level of your true self, you never questioned clarity. All these feelings are just present, so you do not really know about them. But suddenly, as you get compressed and the veiling sets in, you feel certain doubts coming up. You feel the *lack* of clarity. Things are getting foggy. On the level of bliss, on the level of the absolute, *you know that you know.* But on the mental level, you feel that you *don't* know. There is a question mark wherever you look.

What happens if you feel something is lacking? You try to compensate for it, you try to find

113

a surrogate – something that replaces what you feel is lacking. On this level, you are not really clear *what* is lacking, you just feel a lack, something is not quite as it should be. So, you get active and try to replace it. So, what do you do on a mental level to replace clarity? Ah, you try to *control* things. You try to create an environment where you live in and where things work *as you expect*. The more limits you take on, the smaller your world gets, the *less* you can be surprised by the non-control of your environment.

So, if you live in a very small world, full of limitations, very structured, then you have a surrogate for clarity, because things work as you expect.

A lack wants a surrogate. The funny thing is, even if you come to understand this and allow yourself to open up then *still* you want to control. You want to *control the changes*. This is why I say, do not try to control the light body exercise and how the physical body responds. But the mental just *wants* to control, it wants clarity, "What am I doing here, and why am I doing it?" It wants clarity.

Even the scientists, they make a living from *not yet being clear* about things. Can you see that? The scientist conducts research. He *does not know*. The good thing is, most often he knows that he doesn't know. Afterwards, he might pretend that he knows something, or knows enough to do something with it. Like empirically coming to an understanding how certain things work and then they can control and replicate it – and then they are happy. They have clarity, or so they think.

But in reality, what do they have? They have limited themselves to a tiny fraction of what is possible, and then they call it clarity. Control is the substitute for clarity.

On the next level we have love, or unconditional acceptance. This is about the emotional body. So, once you are compressed to that level and take on an emotional body, you have forgotten almost everything. You don't even know anymore *who* you are. So, you make your false identities based on the control patterns that you have created on the mental level. You show somebody the image that you think you are and you beg that the other validates you, likes you, accepts you. So, this is the surrogate for unconditional love: *conditional acceptance.* I will show you a certain face and behavior and I assume that you will validate my behavior.

This is the very reason why groups form. It is not so much because of the deep love or bonding, so often it is just the *sharing of the same illusions and emotional frictions.* They validate each other in their respective state. Thus, they get the surrogate for love, they get conditional acceptance.

Love can be experienced with every being. With *every* being! It is not a matter of gender, age, hormones, or anything. If you just let down all of your guards and the other person lets down all of his guards, then you experience something that can be called love. It is so deep. It is a communion. When this happens to average people... They meet each other, and for whatever reason, they let down their guards, then they call it love. But letting down the guards is very difficult for most people. So, it doesn't take very long until they pull up the guards again. They close the windows, so to speak, and what they have experienced as love now is a *memory*. A memory that they want to repeat. *But love threatens you.* In a sense, identity and love cannot co-exist. Love exists only if the separation is gone and be it only for an instant. Then you experience what is called true love.

So, if two humans meet, they are always lacking love, because they have been compressed and obtained an emotional body. They know they want love, they want nothing more than that, and they search for it *everywhere*. Once in a while they find a partner and – *boom* – there is this moment or even two. They stick together even though they figure that they are not exactly as compatible in daily life as they might have thought after this great moment of love. But they go for the surrogate. They keep the memory of love and hope that it would repeat in the future. All this seems better than not having love at all.

Now imagine this, you have unconditional love on the level of your pure consciousness. Then you restrict yourself to very, very few people – be it your family, your kids, maybe your current partner or even some more partners. You are lacking the unconditional love of all of existence but expect to get it from *very few people* – this just cannot work. You ask a bit too much of those people.

So, mostly everybody at a certain point is either letting go of love, deciding love is not for me, or they settle for conditional acceptance with a partner. That might be fine, it makes life easier, they can share and all the rest of that, but the full letting down of the guards doesn't happen too often any more. This is what happens on the level of the emotional body.

Then we have the physical body. And you might say, *here* it all becomes real. On the upper levels, it might be complicated, it might not be so good to be without love, it might not be so easy to be without clarity, but you can survive it. But on the physical level, it is about *living or dying.* So, you might change all kinds of behaviors, beliefs, and attitudes on the upper levels, and most often it will not kill you or threaten you to death. But as soon as you go on the physical level, *things become real.*

Suddenly, you are dealing with the cells of your body, with the consciousness that is woven into your cells. Even so, you try to compensate for the lack of safety. The body, in essence, is unsafe. You might say this is the very purpose of incarnating! You create the belief of having a body, which is *the* symbol of separation. It has a skin; you are hurt when your skin is touched or penetrated. It will die. You have to be careful with every bite you swallow. The body always shows you that you are an entity within space. *Be careful, it hurts* if you touch your boundaries.

Having a body means you are not safe. You *will* die, sooner or later. You could die *at any* moment! This knowingness is of course suppressed. Dying is for the others, and most people think they will die far into the future. But there is the inherent knowingness that you are *unsafe* in the physical body. So, what do you do? You look for a surrogate. What is it? Well, depending on your culture and your age, you might try to build muscles and acquire fighting skills, or skills to deal with other people. You might hoard money or knowledge. You might build a big house or a fortress around yourself. You might team up with others and build guards, and police forces, and armies. All in an attempt to compensate for the feeling of safety.

But deep down you know, whatever you do, in the end death will catch you. You can pretend you can live without love, okay. You can live without clarity, most certainly. *But you cannot live forever.* Even though you might not want to live forever, you know that you couldn't anyway.

So, you know you are *not* safe, no matter what you do. Thus, you go into denial and suppression. You say, "That's okay for me. I'm fine with death, I have no problem to die." It might even be true on your higher levels of consciousness. Specifically, the more awakened people most certainly have to find a position in respect to death. But, when it comes to letting go of the physical in a conscious way, shifting into the light body, then they truly face death on the level of their cells. And this is something that is *not* easy. It is not simple. If it was, life would be much easier.

So, this is what this life body exercise is all about. What actually happens is, first, you bring forth from the level of your true self the intention of having a light body and with that intention it is instantly there. That's the nature of pure consciousness. The light body is a projection into this world.

Then you bring forth a certain feeling. That feeling floods all of your light body, *all* of your light body, and the light body is all around you and within you. By doing so, it *soothes the lack* that you feel on the various levels of your human existence. This is the idea underlying the light body exercise. It *soothes* you; it makes you calm. You are satisfied on the deepest level *from within* without needing to search on the outside. And to do so, there is *nothing* to do other than shifting your awareness to that certain feeling. By doing so over and over again, it is getting more natural.

So, why not just do the light body exercise.

*

[Music plays]

First and foremost, as always, really become aware of your physical body in its totality. Take

119

on the position of clarity, of royalty. What you are going to do is the *highest* a human can do. Never forget that. So there is grace in it. There is beauty in it. Take on a position of beauty and grace, simplicity, royalty. Stretch the backbone and just breathe. Let the breathing come and go. *Do not control* your breath. Do not try to breathe long or deep or anything... just let it come and go.

As you get used to it, as you repeat this over and over again, you will come to the point where you can simply observe what is going on without being trapped in it. Whenever you notice you are sucked back into it, you just step out again.

You might even imagine your true self being with you in this exercise. Your true self has an interest in this. So even on your bad days, where things are just crazy and your mind and emotions and chemicals are doing their dance, when you feel nothing is going forward, be sure that your true self is on your side. It is with you. It is you. It wants you.

So, when you come to a state of calmness within you, *know*, just know that your light body is all around you and permeating you. It is there as an intention on the level of cause, on the level of the true self.

Now, I will suggest a small tool. You do not have to use it, but you might want to experiment with it. It is about bringing forth a feeling and then to intensify that feeling. To give you the impression that you can increase the intensity up to the point that your physical body is ready to accept, imagine a dimmer knob. A dimmer like you use to regulate the brightness of a lamp. As you turn the dimmer, you intensify gradually the feeling that you choose to bring forth in that given moment.

But the dimmer is a bit special, it works exponentially. This means, whenever you turn it up a notch, it increases the current intensity tenfold. So, a small turning of the dimmer results in the feeling's intensity times ten.

Remember when we went out to the sun? We came there from the human condition, and suddenly we were faced with millions of degrees. It was no problem at that moment. But let's see what it means if we do that while being more focused in the physical and bringing forth such an enormous intensity. We do this so the light body can outshine everything within it, which is the physical, and then the physical will mimic it. Also, the consciousness that is hypnotized into believing it is physical will slowly start to wake up. It will remember.

So, let's start with the feeling of safety. Here, in this workshop, you are used to being safe, so maybe it's easiest to imagine a situation that is not so safe, like, say, you are sitting in an airplane, and there are heavy turbulences. You are getting shaken up, falling a few meters until the airplane stabilizes again. This is certainly not a feeling of safety, but of being *unsafe*. Compared to being in that airplane, sitting here feels very safe, right?

Just be aware of that feeling of safety. Let it flow through your light body and do not try to control what your physical body does. This is most important. Your physical body will *always* react, and as soon as your body reacts, you want to control it. That's the way it is. Get *used to not controlling* your physical body while doing this exercise.

Whenever you sense body reactions, there is also a tendency to even think, "Wow, great, it works! I'm doing it!" Let that go. Yes, it is exciting, but the excitement will disturb the whole process.

You just remain with the light body. In a sense, on a certain level you shift your consciousness into the light body, and the physical body will do its thing to mimic its surrounding.

So, let's feel safety.

Ah, safety. The human is *never* safe. Never, ever. But now, there is safety. Nothing can harm you. *Nothing.* The light body is *yours.* One can say, nothing has access to it *but you.*

It doesn't consist of energy. It does not need to bring in anything – it just is in suchness. So safe.

Now increase the intensity by turning the dimmer, make it more intense. It is *safe!* It is not a dream, it is true. Allow your physical body to relax, to rejoice. Ah – safety. The cells always fight for survival, all the time. And now there is safety.

Turn the dimmer up a notch. Intensify safety –
times ten. Not just a little bit, but times ten. You
see, by doing this, you release the doubt. You can
even say, as you intensify a given feeling, you go
towards bliss and into pure consciousness. And
nothing, as we know, can withstand pure consciousness. The doubt just vanishes into the light
of your pure consciousness.

Safety. Feel it. Try to be aware of all of your
light body. By doing so, you are also present in
all of your physical body without doing it
actively. You are aware within your light body.

How long has it been since you have felt really
safe? How long? How hard do you try to be safe,
in every moment of your day?

If you are bold, use the dimmer. Turn it – times
ten. *Unfathomable safety.* Safety beyond any
doubt.

Do not track your body reactions. Do not.
Tracking them pulls you back into the physical.
Let go of the biology. It was made for this.

There is only one exception to this. If you get
the clear signal "no more intensity" then you follow it. There is no reason to be quick or to *push*
anything. If it is too much, it's okay. Just decrease
the intensity.

This is the desensitizing I spoke of. You want
to stay here in this world with pure consciousness,
but pure consciousness is intense. Remember the

consciousness implosion? Well, we are approaching these energies and intensities, but this time as a liberation.

Next, love. You all have felt love, at least once. It doesn't matter if it was a person, or a pet, a parent, or even nature. There was a deep feeling of communion, a letting go of all of your guards, a beautiful moment. Maybe it was even your very first romantic love when you were twelve years old, innocent, pure. So beautiful. Now feel that love, and let your light body be full of this love. You are surrounded by it, from the top to the bottom, everywhere. You might get the shivers and all the rest of that – do not track them. Be aware of them.

Your emotional body instantly, instantly, instantly reacts. It is confused. What is going on? It didn't do anything. It didn't beg, didn't act, didn't play, didn't force, didn't push – suddenly there is love that it craves so much! Oh, the false identities are confused. What's going on? Love, just like this? Me!?

Can you imagine what that does to your physical body? If your emotional body is soothed by bringing forth a feeling of unconditional love within? Can you even imagine all the influence it has on the physical body? All the stress is going away. What does that mean in relation to illnesses?

But this is not about *curing* anything. This may come as a byproduct. This is not done to *achieve* anything. This is *not* a doing.

Feel love, then turn the dimmer up. Love, times ten.

Ask yourself, what was the longest period of love you have ever experienced? And be honest. Was it more than a few seconds before it was replaced with memories and wishes and hopes?

But here you have love. From yourself for yourself, for all of yourself. The purest love. Unconditional, *unconditional*! You do not need to do anything to deserve it or earn it. It's yours.

Now, if you are so bold, take your dimmer and turn it. Love, times ten, once again... and the doubt goes away. Why go out there and search for anything to replace *this* kind of love with conditional acceptance?

Do you know what? There is no reason to ever let go of this love. This is *yours*. It was just *veiled*. It was always there; it was just veiled by means of the compression.

Now, with the wisdom and the understanding, you release the veil. You find what was always yours.

I want to inject another feeling, which is my favorite. This is *beauty*. It doesn't correspond to a single level of your existence, but I love it so much, I bring it in. Beauty. Feel beauty.

Love is beautiful, isn't it?

When you feel beauty, in a sense, *everything stops!* That's the wonder of beauty. You go somewhere, and suddenly you discover something beautiful, and time stands still. Suddenly, it is just you and the beauty. You come around a corner, here in Cascais, and suddenly you see the ocean – ah, beautiful.

That beauty is already within. Now, beauty times ten.

Ah, it is so special. Beauty is... universal. It doesn't correspond so much to the human. You can live without beauty, but if it's there – *it's so beautiful.*

Once again, turn the dimmer. Beauty times ten.

Isn't it interesting? The beauty that you feel right now doesn't even need expression. It doesn't need to be brought into a form. Sure, it could. But everything beautiful you see outside is just a remembrance of your innate beauty. It *reminds* you of your true self. The ocean, out there, in all of its beauty, reminds you of your beauty within that is always there.

Now we come to clarity. Clarity. When was the last time that you have been really clear, *really* clear? Maybe yesterday? Within the Trinity? There was a moment where all of the questions were gone. You didn't have the answers, but why would you need answers if there are no questions? This is clarity. This is the *I know that I know.*

With clarity, you can let go of the need to control. Can you imagine that? *Not* trying to control what is going on all around you? How long ago was that? I know that I know. I do not need to control.

Turn the dimmer. Clarity, times ten.

It spreads out. You see, in a sense, the physical body is very limited in space. The emotional body is larger than the physical body, but still limited. The mental body, in a way, is huge, really huge. You might say, it is unlimited. But it has been confined into a controlled space, where your thoughts were of your liking. Always the same, okay, but at least you knew them. If you let go of control, you suddenly feel a vastness. A vastness that is not measured in space, but a vastness of potential thoughts.

You become aware of other realities. You do not need to control so much anymore. You are safe, you do not need anything. Then you can allow yourself to perceive, no need to filter out anything – if you so choose. Clarity. So vast.

Once again, turn your dimmer. Clarity, times ten.

Your light body is full of clarity. From your feet to your skull, and within. Without any limitation.

From here, let's go to bliss. You see, we have built up from the bottom to the top, with safety, love, beauty, and clarity. They are all combined already. Let's go to bliss. All the beautiful feelings a human can have, combined into bliss. No need to name them all. Just feel bliss.

Let the bliss flood your light body. Feel safety, and love, and beauty, and clarity – all simultaneously. Add completion, freedom, serenity, peace, joy – it's all there, it's yours. It has always been. Now you allow yourself to become aware of it again without any outer stimulation. Just by choice.

Turn your dimmer. Bliss, times ten.

This is so beautiful to witness. Can you see how easy it is? All that we have talked about culminates in such a simple practice. In a way, it brings it all together. Except one thing – and this is the consciousness that is hypnotized into thinking it is physical. The only way this can be released is through yourself. No one can do it for you.

Yesterday, I asked you to find the vibration of your true self, you might call it your name. It's a resonance, a light, a feeling. It is bliss enriched by all the experiences you ever had in separation. This is your unique signature. This is *you*. Now send *that* into your light body.

You see, bliss is universal. But when enriched with your experiences, by the *wisdom* coming from your experiences – *this is you*. And nobody is like you.

Your signature contains the remembrance of your very first realization of "I exist". It even contains the remembrance of when you decided to incarnate. As this vibration, this resonance, is fully present in your light body, it goes deep, deep, deep into the physical. It gently touches the consciousness that has been split apart and is deeply sleeping. This is the wake-up call.

But you needed to be ready to allow it, you see? You cannot just go around and tell people about this – they wouldn't listen. They couldn't understand and what's more, there is something odd with human consciousness. If a wisdom, a true wisdom, is rejected once, it usually doesn't get a second chance. It takes another lifetime... or maybe an alternate expression.

This is why the deepest, deepest initiations are the simplest, and they come at the very end.

Can you accept the simplicity?

Do not push anything. You can slowly intensify the vibration of your name within the light body, even times ten. Do not push. But if you remember yesterday, when we visited an atom, you might feel the consciousness on that level and how it is waking up.

Here you are, in the full bliss of pure consciousness, enriched with all the wisdom you have ever distilled from your experiences, a sovereign being. *Sovereign.* You can gently wake up and release the physical, and the physical will now become your friend, truly your friend. You are not chained to it any more, not magnetized to it, hypnotized into it. It becomes a friend. It becomes an extension of you.

The roles reverse, you see. For so long you have thought, here is your physical body and there is your light body, and you were 99.9% of the time in the physical, only once in a while having access to your light body. Now you allow this to change.

As you repeat this exercise, you will shift into the light body. This will become your center of existence, here, in this dream world of separation. Your physical body will become a friend, an extension. It will follow your intents. For in the end, this is what dreams are – they are all your intents.

Do not think in terms of time. When you do this exercise, you are beyond time. You do not question anything. All is just perfect as it is. Maybe you can hold this state and make it your normal state, but be honest with yourself. Going into the grocery store, fighting with your kids or your boss, being in the traffic... this is difficult. It will take time, but as we know *time does not matter.*

The only thing that is required is shifting your perspective towards the Eye of Suchness. In the end, what we are currently doing *is* the Eye of Suchness. It contains everything.

*

You would not want to speak about this with an average person, for they will not understand. They will belittle it. It might create doubt within you. Some *might* understand, and you will know it. Then you can talk about it, in your own terms. The background, why this works, can be very helpful. You can omit it, it works even without the knowingness of that, but having an understanding of the background is a way to appease the mind, the questioning mind and the searcher.

But it's so important to really understand, *this*

is not an exercise of well-being and then to jump into the pool of separation to have fun.

This is the way out. This is the going beyond.

You might say, a moment like we are having right now, when you are fully in your light body, in bliss enriched with the resonance of your true self, having integrated the physical – *this is a moment of embodied ascension.*

Just like it is with enlightenment, it happens always moment by moment, for this is the way that separation is structured. It is moment by moment, sphere by sphere.

In a sense, you have to bring it forth in each sphere that you enter. It cannot be tomorrow, it will not be yesterday, it's always in the now.

Your presence is always in the now. Your enlightenment is always in the now, and embodied ascension *is always in the now.*

Embodied ascension is *not a fruit* of your practice. It is in the now, full and complete unto itself.

*

I have no reason to leave, and in a sense, I won't. I will maintain a memory of this specific sphere of separation and admire the beauty for as long as I wish. But, as you are doing this embodied ascension thing, I will kind of leave you now and I'll stay with you. The dragon you brought forth yesterday will stay with you also. There are even those from the other side that are with you, if you so choose. Members of Uru and others. They'll accompany you, comfort you. If you need companions, well, just go out and ask – they will be there. Or call your buddy from this workshop with skype and have a chat.

We will let the music continue playing for a while, and we'll see you tomorrow.

I am Althar, the Crystal Dragon.

7. The End of Separation – Rebirth – Ila

I am Althar, the Crystal Dragon!

So here we are. Ready, for the finale. Me personally, Althar, I have been looking forward to this very moment. To this very moment in my own career with you, and to this moment in which I will bring forth a message that I have agreed to convey.

So, I invite you to really feel into this moment, and bring together *all* that has been said in the last few days here, all that has been said in the books, and all the wisdom that you have gathered elsewhere. Take a moment, bring it all together within you, and then we will start from there.

[Music plays]

*

This will be a very, very personal moment. Right now, we are completely beyond time. Completely beyond your linear time that you might have before you in your human life. Here we are in a moment of eternity. A moment that, in a sense, has already happened, that happens all the time, and that will be available even after time has vanished.

It is your personal moment, and we are here to preview it. You might feel this as, say, a movie within yourself that goes very deep, but at a certain point in your linear lifetime, you will re-experience a version of this moment. Even more personal than now, and then you will truly fathom what today you might have only glimpsed at.

This is a personal moment, and in this personal moment, I do not speak to a group. I only speak to *you* who is hearing me right now. I do not speak to the person that seems to sit to your left or to your right. I only speak to you who is hearing me right now.

I come to you as a voice that you have invited. Invited to remind you of something that you have kind of forgotten while traversing the worlds of separation.

When being so deeply in matter, in the physical, one tends to forget the grandiosity of oneself. So, often times, it is easier if a truth comes from the outside, or *apparently* from the outside. Thus, you allowed my voice to be with you in this personal moment.

If you truly feel into this personal moment, you might also feel Ila. Ila, the unborn Goddess of Female Beingness. Also known as the Goddess of Bliss. Ila is here, for Ila represents a part of you that never entered separation. Ila reminds you of that part of you that was never birthed, that has always been within, what I call the expanding perfection of pure consciousness.

Ila has been forgotten. Whoever enters the worlds of separation, the dream of separation, is biased towards what you call the masculine. Even if you carry a female body, you are always biased towards the masculine. You have to. For you are in separation. In separation, you want to survive. You have to apply separation. You *have* to! Otherwise, you cannot walk through separation, live in separation, experience in separation. But a portion of you which equals Ila did not come with you. In a way, Ila bid you farewell when you left.

Take some time to feel that.

*

Ila, the part of you that never entered separation, that is from a human perspective totally untarnished, pure *absolutely pure*. She has no intents. She doesn't want anything. She is just in the expanding perfection. She is with you in your personal moment. A moment of rebirth. A moment where you allow yourself to be rebirthed.

Let us, once again, make a trip toward my favorite place, the sun. Let's just be there instantly and have a look at the Earth from the perspective of the sun.

See the beauty.

Many of you have the experience of having held a baby, in your arms or hands. Holding a baby, an entity full of potentials, is a very beautiful thing.

Now, imagine you hold the whole Earth in your arms, in your hands, and feel that.

That's beyond beauty.

Once you fully allow the knowingness, the true wisdom, that the belief in separation is not real, you come to see all the worlds and realms of separation as one entity.

You do not consider your physical body to be an aggregation of individual cells. It is one. You see it as one organism.

As you look upon Earth, she becomes one organism, including all the entities living there. Yes, they might seem to fight, or to love. They are playing their games in separation. But seen from here, it becomes one organism of beauty, of expression, of experience.

Be with that for a moment. Allow that feeling to settle.

*

I have a question for you: If there is no separation, where does the inside end and where does the outside begin?

So many humans are striving for enlightenment. They have heard the call. They came to the conclusion that repetition cannot be the *real thing*. Yet, usually they spend so much time, so many lifetimes, just to create a better personal life, to gain more control. They wish for skills to fulfill their wishes. They want validation, even of their spiritual self.

When they come to the point where they realize that separation *is not real*, they shy away. Even if they have overcome all the obstacles that we have talked about. The false identities, the patterns, guilt, shame, fear. Even if they have overcome all of this, still there is something to shy away from. Because if separation is not real, reality breaks through – and this can be overwhelming.

So, they go back. They have sneaked in and have been overpowered, because here for the very first time they have come in contact with the *true power*. They might have searched power in separation in the terms of being able to push energies, to dominate or manipulate things or beings. But here they feel the true power. The true power of a creator. That's huge! Especially if you have spent eons, and eons, and eons of time having forgotten what true power is.

Thus I say, this very personal moment is, in a way, a movie that we are playing, or that you are playing for yourself, in order to prepare yourself.

So, dear one, I ask you again: *If there is no separation, where does the inside end and where does the outside begin?*

Where does the sun end and the Earth begin?

Can you *fathom* the truth?

Can you *embrace* it?

Can you even *embody* it?

So, let me state the obvious: If there is no separation, then obviously *you are your own universe,* and by universe I do not just mean the physical universe. I mean All-That-Is.

In your universe, you are the only ruler. So, can you take responsibility for what happens in your universe?

You are the stars and the galaxies. You are the earth, the wind, the oceans, the plants, the animals, and in a way even the humans.

A being who approaches sovereignty, his true heritage, *has to see things as they truly are!* And, actually, *what you see is truly you!*

If you see with the eye of separation, you always create borders. You make distinctions between me and not-me. Me and the object you see. Thus, I say: You are not what you can perceive.

But seen with the Eye of Suchness, separation vanishes, and you know there is no distinction between what you see and the seer. In a sense, there is unity.

*

Allow Ila to become more present.

She joins with the resonance and vibration of your true self, of your true beingness, of your true nature. She comes with the music. She doesn't need words. She is you, has always been. She welcomes you. You are back home. Ila truly knows you have never left for this was but a dream. Seen from beyond time, your dream lasted not even an instant, it was an idea.

Within the dream, you created the perception

of time, of space, of entities and entities and entities – but you played within yourself all the time, in a way.

Just let Ila flow into you, into what you might call your light body, but your light body truly has no inside and no outside. The light body is All-That-Is, and Ila is right there.

*

You might feel how some things shift within you as you remember Ila. In a sense, she is the missing part, the unbirthed part, the female part that does not make distinctions. It is birthing, giving life, but life beyond separation. This is called *true creation.*

*

Allow Ila and yourself to shine this knowingness into all the now-spheres of separation that you might traverse in your human body in the time to come.

You see, you do not change separation, for separation, in a way, is already finished. It is completed. But you project that knowingness into the spheres that you encounter. So, wherever you are henceforth as a human, you have access to this knowingness. You might use the light body all around you as a remembrance when you walk with the physical body. No need to make it as large as the whole universe, although you could. Sometimes this would be a bit cumbersome. But, just walk within your light body and know who you truly are and see what suddenly happens! For you become more and more free.

Can you imagine doing something without requiring a return effect, a mirroring? Doing something just for doing it! A deed that is completed in itself, because *you* are already completed. That is a blessing of enlightenment: *Knowing that you are complete unto yourself – already!* Even though seen from within the physical body, it might not always seem that way.

But still, as you continue to let go of patterns, beliefs that still linger here and there, the clarity becomes greater and greater. The knowingness of who you truly are becomes greater and greater. Suddenly, the understanding that separation is just a dream is natural. It is not an idea, or a hope, or a belief. It is a true wisdom that liberates instantly.

*

Now the question comes up: Are there other true selves?

Yes, in a way, and they even interact.

You see, each of the true selves are equal. They are all their own universe, but they interact. So, if two humans meet on the street, there are two universes interacting. Each is projecting an image of the other into its own universe and interprets it the way he likes, as a mirror. You never see the real person. It's always your perceptions, colored by your emotions, your mind, and your memories.

That is true for everybody. When they interact, there is no common playground in terms of space. But there are agreements about how to represent each other so that they may come to insights.

Now, if a human being comes to enlightenment and continues walking in a physical body, you might say that person in a sense stops mirroring the other. It becomes like a *hole* in the universe of the other. It can be felt that there is something, but it is not reacting by the ways of separation, by the ways of cause and effect. It is just there in total acceptance. Not even reflecting, and *this* can be felt. This is the *scent* of Ila, the *scent* of enlightenment, the *scent* of the call for enlightenment.

You have noticed it, over and over again. That's why you are here. You cannot even say where and when you have noticed it. Thus, it is so important, if you so choose, to stay a while and, in a way, spread the news, to make it easier for others. For you know, indeed *you* know, that traversing separation is not only a ride in beauty. It contains a lot of suffering and frustration.

*

I talked about pure energy in one of my very first messages. I said, pure energy is a slight, slight transmutation of your pure consciousness. So, it is still *your* consciousness. Pure energy reflects your intents, and when the intent is to explore separation, it does so. We have seen that with the intent of separation, separation is instantly created in totality. You just choose certain now-spheres to experience, and they all play out within your pure energy – *which is you!* It does not take any space. It does not.

There is no physical energy. It is all played out within your pure energy. When I said, "A dragon guides energy", we can now translate it into, "A dragon highlights now-spheres to visit." It can just highlight them.

So, a dragon might highlight a now-sphere where there is more liberation, and you might choose to go there. Then, from the inside, it feels as if energy has guided you.

In a way, you might say, the whole dream collapses. All the universes suddenly become very small, for how big is a true self? It has no size. Feel into that, into the *simplicity*.

*

Another question might come up: How many true selves are there? How many?

Let's be honest. In the light of what I have said, one true self would suffice, wouldn't it? For if separation comes into existence instantly, there is no need for any "other". You could have created all the seemingly existing entities.

Now feel into this: Imagine, you would be the *only* true self in all of existence. You would be the pure consciousness that is and nothing else is. Feel into that.

*

Oh, I can feel what you feel. It feels lonely, doesn't it?

If you were the only true self in all of existence, maybe, just maybe, you would ponder to have an offspring. Another to share with. And maybe, just maybe, it was the pondering of the *impossible*, namely separation, that was the means to bring forth this offspring.

So, parts and pieces of pure consciousness entered separation. Each of them having unique experiences and their very personal, personal, personal thread of time and even no-time. They had so many experiences, thereby taking on certain characteristics, becoming kind of different entities. And maybe, just maybe, with pondering the impossible, separation, a thought was sent with it. A thought that this is not *really* real. A knowingness that came to you *in so many* forms. As sages, as angels, as gods, as insights, through words such as you are hearing right now. And maybe you could call this knowingness even an "Ambassador of Creation".

Feel into that.

Maybe, just maybe, this one true self knew that at some point those equals of him, his offspring, would come out of separation, joining back with pure consciousness, but enriched by all their experiences which in a sense gave them unique characteristics. So, it can be said that they are *unique in unity*.

143

They are all rays of the one I Am.

Each offspring, of course, has the full creator capabilities for *it is* the creator.

Then, this offspring could share the joy of bringing forth true creation. *True creation!* No repetition, no separation.

But... who knows for sure? Where the true selves came from is kind of a mystery. But pondering the mystery can sometimes be very interesting, and it might even happen that you touch upon the truth.

Feel that. But no matter how the true selves came into existence, at some point they will go beyond separation. They will rediscover their true heritage of being a sovereign creator, and the moment they do so, they take note of the others that are with them. Some still in the dream of separation, others already ascended.

What a joy.

*

This is a personal moment.

Letting go of separation is not just a mind game. It is the only thing that you can actually do within separation. All the rest is just jumping from sphere to sphere.

If you are true to yourself, then you'll see that in each and every moment, you have only one choice as a human being, as an incarnated being, as *any* being in separation: How do you want to perceive reality? Do you want to perceive it with the eye of separation and therefore, solidify separation, making it more real? Or do you want to see it with the Eye of Suchness? *Seeing it as it truly is.* There is no right or wrong answer to that. It is *your* choice. It is *your* freedom in each and every moment. Instant for instant, in each and every now-sphere. Therefore, there is not this single now-sphere of importance. It's available to you always and always.

*

Remember this moment. At some point, you will relive it in a personal version. But do not chase it. It will come to you. When it comes, you will be ready to embrace all that you are. You will be ready to embrace the true power of creation. You will *know* that because you have let go of *all* fear, guilt, and shame that you will not misuse it – because by then you will have understood that there is nothing that you *could* misuse in the first place.

Prior to that, you are still hanging on to the notion of physical energies, trying to improve things.

Doing the light body exercise will help you get accustomed to the intensity of the feelings. Remember the compression? You open up to all that you are.

I mean, look around. All that you see is also creation. Isn't that beautiful? Even in separation. Now imagine what creation is *without* separation?

And this is *you*, the *true you*.

Imagine, if you want to think in terms of energy, how much energy you use every split second to maintain all the boundaries that you want to see. *Can you imagine that?* Boundaries everywhere! How much energy is required for this? And all of this energy suddenly becomes available, all that consciousness is suddenly freed.

*

You have come a long, long way, dear friend, seen from within time.

Seen from the perspective of pure consciousness, you have never ever been away.

*

Ila represents the part of you that was never in the dream. That part of you will remain with you. Oh, it will *not* enter the dream. *By no means!* But *now* you can perceive it, you can be *aware* of it. It is your personal bridge in consciousness, always, always available to you.

*

Have a look from this perspective onto your human life that you think you will have to live.

There is no need to change anything.

If you feel you have to take care of anything, kids, parents, pets, no matter what, the plants, the whales, the oceans – you might do that. But now you are free in doing so. You do not want a response. Can you imagine how much easier your life will be? How much more of help you can be, if you so choose?

This then is embodied ascension. Walking the light, walking pure consciousness in a physical body, yet knowing who you truly are.

This changes everything.

This personal moment will never end. It is there for eternity, for it is a *true creation*. It will even expand. It will get deeper and deeper for you. And in some moment along your future thread of time, you will just stand in the midst of it, full of joy, not being overwhelmed, and you will know:

This is true reality.

*

Slowly come back to your human body here in this gathering. We have been accompanied by *many,* by many from the other side.

Every letting go changes all of existence. Can you imagine that? It loosens separation for all that is.

We are amongst the first who are doing this consciously. The impact is monumental.

No matter what you do, no matter how tiny you think your role is – it is *monumental.*

Never forget that.

And never forget the one choice you have: The choice for the Eye of Suchness.

Stay in this room for a while. The music will play. Embrace your physical body. Integrate the moment we have just shared.

I am Althar, an Ambassador of Creation.

Acknowledgment

I would like to express my heartfelt gratitude to Nazar Fedunkiv for creating the initial transcript and to Lynn Halladay, Nina Spitzer, and Jennifer Walsh-Rupakheti for proofreading the final version. Thanks to all of you!

Made in the USA
Monee, IL
04 September 2023

42106984R00090